SLIM CUISINE: INDULGENT DESSERTS

SUE KREITZMAN

—— Cambridge ——

Slim Cuisine:
Indulgent Desserts

BANTAM PRESS

LONDON · NEW YORK · TORONTO · SYDNEY · AUCKLAND

TRANSWORLD PUBLISHERS LTD
61–63 Uxbridge Road, London W5 5SA

TRANSWORLD PUBLISHERS (AUSTRALIA) PTY LTD
15–23 Helles Avenue, Moorebank, NSW 2170

TRANSWORLD PUBLISHERS (NZ) LTD
Cnr Moselle and Waipareira Aves,
Henderson, Auckland

Published 1991 by Bantam Press
a division of Transworld Publishers Ltd
Copyright © Sue Kreitzman 1991

Photographs by Sue Atkinson
China used courtesy of Token House-Windsor

The right of Sue Kreitzman to be identified
as author of this work has been asserted in accordance
with sections 77 and 78 of the Copyright Designs and
Patents Act 1988.

A catalogue record for this book is available
from the British Library.
ISBN hardcover 0593 021991
trade paperback 0593 022009

Phototypeset in Palatino by Chippendale Type Ltd.,
Otley, West Yorkshire
Printed in Great Britain
by Mackays of Chatham Plc, Chatham, Kent

To my dear, chocolate-loving friends,
Margaret and Terry Pedersen.

Acknowledgements:

Many, many thanks to my secretary, chocoholic-supremo Rose-marie Espley, and to my talented assistant, Sandie Perry. Thanks as well to their families, who were always willing to taste an unlimited number of new Slim Cuisine desserts, and then give the recipes the thumbs-up, or thumbs-down. Thanks, too, to helper Brenda Huebler whose hard work ensures that we do not become mired in chaos. Brenda's family also served as intrepid tasters, and Brenda contributed a recipe of her own, Strawberry Frozen Yoghurt. And thank you to helper Mary Hardy who is, by now, practically a member of the family.

I am deeply grateful to Dr Alan N. Howard and the Howard Foundation for their support of my research and to my husband, Dr Stephen Kreitzman. Under the tutelage of Dr Husband, I have been able to breathe the rarefied air of international obesity research.

Alison Campbell at Panasonic has been generous with advice on the role of the microwave in dessert cookery, and was kind enough to loan me a machine for testing purposes.

Sue Atkinson, with the help of Carol Handslip, produced a set of photographs that outstripped even her usual brilliant efforts: I am in awe of her ability to give my recipes such pulsating and vivid photographic life.

I am delighted with Giles Johnson's vivid cover portrait of me and my kitchen, and with Lizzy Laczynska and Bipin Patel, who – as usual – have designed a beautiful volume.

Fervid thanks to Bantam editor Ursula Mackenzie and her assistants, Alison Tulett and Broo Doherty. Their calm good nature is much appreciated.

And to my son Shawm, who thinks that Slim Cuisine Chocolate Sorbet is one of life's ultimates, thanks for making *my* life so interesting.

' . . . they fail to see the art in ordinary things: in her cheesecakes and banana bread, bran muffins, white and dark bread, chocolate chip and oatmeal cookies, rhubarb and apple and cherry pies. What is it if not art, to take ingredients not necessarily useful or desirable on their own and combine them into works of a certain symmetry and grace and usefulness? And not only that: because while painters might look at their work and sculptors touch theirs, she could do that and consume hers also, containing her own art.'

Joan Barfoot, *Duet for Three*

Contents

Introduction

Puddings and desserts figure strongly in memories of childhood's golden culinary moments. In my travels around the UK and the US, whenever I ask people to share recipes and food memories with me (and I do ask – tirelessly), the subject of puddings comes up again and again. From Canada to Mexico, from John o'Groats to Land's End, folks remember with deep fondness a sweet that was served to them in childhood by a mother or grandmother or aunt. Whether it is the custard-soaked, raisin-studded voluptuousness of an English bread pudding, the legendary velvet creaminess of a New York cheesecake, the supernal hot and cold comfort of a hot fudge sundae, the mashed-bread-and-berry juiciness of a scarlet summer pudding, or the homely sugar-sprinkled stodginess of a fruit-filled dumpling, it is inevitably described with an almost tearful intensity.

For those who blossom into billowing fat at the mere mention of cream, butter, eggs and excess sugar, pudding nostalgia can be a nightmare. Are fat-prone adults doomed to suffer? Must we choose one: the desserts of yesteryear, or obesity? Advice is flung at us from all sides. For instance: 'Eat small portions only. Don't be such a pig!' What utter rubbish! Small portions are agonizing – and what *is* a small portion for that matter? Fat people (and ex-fat people) have trouble defining this concept. Exactly how small is small? Do we have to whip out a ruler and a postage scale to make sure our measly dab of allowed pud is exactly the right size? By the time we finish weighing and measuring and scrutinizing, any spontaneous gastronomic joy we may have gleaned from our pitiful serving is gone. And with the tastes and textures of that small serving lingering on our palate and in our minds, how do we spend the rest of the evening, how do we relax, how do we sleep, when the remaining pudding waits in its dish, sending out seductive messages that only we seem to hear?

How about that other piece of dubious advice that I've heard flung in our direction : 'Don't eat pudding at all – have a piece of underripe fruit instead, while we lucky thin ones attack the pudding.' Or even worse: 'Don't fret – you may eat this beautiful cheesecake, specially constructed for you from tofu and saccharine. You may feast on this ever so nice "chocolate" mousse fabricated from carob and powdered, pasteurized egg whites. Aren't *you* the lucky one!'

Give me a break! Save me from the thin advisers. It's true that I'm determined to protect my health, and *never be fat again*, but I still want lavishness, deep taste and excitement in my culinary encounters. This desire has impelled me to attempt to 'reinvent' cuisine. It has been necessary to throw out many of the basics, dependent as they are (and have been for long centuries) on fats and oils. New techniques have had to be developed to ensure that the food is not insipid. Usually, when fat goes out, so does flavour. My new techniques ensure that flavour (and culinary excitement) *does not* vanish. Slim Cuisine, my system of very low-fat cookery, is sumptuous, delicious, seductive – all those things conventional very low-fat food is *not*.

What fun I've had applying my lateral thinking to puddings and desserts, especially those fraught with nostalgia. All the things I thought I wouldn't be able to do, I *have* done. Cheesecakes? You won't believe them. Creamy, with a crunchy base, they put many conventional killer cheesecakes to shame. Rice pudding, fudgy chocolate brownies, ice cream, towering cakes, pies, flans, tortes, chocolate pudding . . . I'm talking total delight here. And – believe it – not a speck of carob, not a dollop of tofu in sight. (I ask you – would I do such a thing to you?) These desserts are the real thing. They taste rich, creamy, chocolatey – even deeply decadent – but they all contribute significantly to a healthy, very low-fat (and low sugar) life-style. Oh brave new world!

Some Facts about Ingredients

SUGAR

Once, not too many years ago, sugar was blamed for a bewildering host of human ailments, from blindness to heart disease, from tooth decay to extreme depression, from diabetes to gallstones. Since those days, the scientific wind has changed direction and sugar paranoia is no longer with us. Tooth decay is about the only problem laid at sugar's door these days, and even that is tempered with common sense. No longer is the amount of sugar in a particular food considered the sole predictor of its tooth-decaying effect. Frequency of carbohydrate consumption, texture and food particle size are factors that seem to play a major role in the production of dental decay. As far as overweight is concerned, fat, at 9 Calories per gram, is much more of a problem than sugar at 4. Still, sugar's 4 Calories per gram are 'empty' Calories, that is, sugar provides food energy (Calories) and nothing else. As a result, sugar should be used intelligently. The natural sugar you consume in fresh fruits and vegetables works in concert with the valuable nutrients (vitamins, minerals, trace minerals, and fibre) found in those fruits and vegetables, so that the foodstuff is both highly nutritious *and* delicious. Take a tip from nature, and use sugar *sparingly* in your recipes along with as many valuable nutrients as possible. Nutrient density coupled with lovely flavour is what good cooking is all about.

Brown sugars, unrefined sugars and honey are no more nutritious than plain white sugar. It's true that unrefined sugar and honey contain tiny amounts of vitamins and minerals while white sugar contains none at all. But the operant word here is *tiny*. Unrefined sugar and honey would have to be consumed in enormous quantities in order for their traces of nutrients to contribute significantly to daily requirements. For instance, it would take more than 3 pints of honey (8,000 Calories worth!) to come close to meeting a woman's daily requirement for riboflavin.

That is not to say that the fat-prone person should avoid honey at all costs. It has a lovely taste, and sweetens beautifully: in fact, it is sweeter than white sugar, and so can be used in slightly smaller quantities. Just remember: honey is – essentially – just another form of sugar, and as such, contains virtually empty Calories. Use it with prudence. And if you are trying to *lose* weight, as opposed to maintaining, cut out sugars (including honey) altogether.

ASPARTAME (NutraSweet)

NutraSweet is a very low-Calorie sweetener. It is extremely valuable when you are trying to lose weight, and want to cut down on sugar's empty Calories. NutraSweet is synthesized from two amino acids (amino acids are the building blocks of protein), is 200 times sweeter than sugar, and has no bitter aftertaste. You can buy granulated NutraSweet in large jars. Unfortunately, it cannot be used successfully in baked desserts, or in *any* dessert that needs to be heated. It does not react in baking the way sugar does, and besides, when heated, most of its sweetness dissipates. It is extremely useful, however, in ice creams, sorbets, cold dessert sauces, milkshakes, and so on. If you want to *lose* weight, stick to recipes that use NutraSweet. When you are *maintaining*, you may use sugar some of the time, and NutraSweet some of the time. It is never a good idea to overload on either one.

VANILLA

The lovely aroma and flavour of natural vanilla are essential to many of the recipes in this collection. Use vanilla in your dessert cookery in one of the following ways:

1   **Bottled natural vanilla essence or natural vanilla extract.** Don't ever buy synthetic vanilla flavouring; it is harsh and unpleasant. The best pure vanilla extracts and essences are the French and American ones (see Mail Order Guide, page 133).

2   **Vanilla beans.** The vanilla bean is the fruit of an orchid, *Vanilla planifolia.* You can buy the long, thin, black pods in jars (one per jar) from the herb and spice shelf in many supermarkets. If you slit open the vanilla pod lengthwise with a sharp paring knife you will see (and smell) that it is filled with a hauntingly aromatic pulp. Scrape out the black pulp with the tip of your knife, and use it in ice creams, custards, and puddings of all sorts. *Do not* throw away the scraped pod! Use it in vanilla sugar and vanilla NutraSweet (see below).

3   **Vanilla NutraSweet and vanilla sugar.** Bury a whole vanilla pod or scraped-out vanilla pod in a jar of NutraSweet or a canister of sugar. After a few days, the sweetener will be imbued with the vanilla flavour. When the sweeteners are used up, save the pod. It will last for many jars of NutraSweet, or canisters of sugar.

DAIRY PRODUCTS

To switch from Fat Cuisine to Slim Cuisine, you must change your supermarket strategy. On the Slim Cuisine regime there are certain things you *do not* buy: butter, margarine, 'low-fat' spreads, cream, sour cream, full-fat or part-skimmed milk, or – indeed – any full fat or part-skimmed dairy product. Fortunately, there are many excellent skimmed milk products available: simply get into the habit of buying them instead of the old Fat Cuisine ingredients.

Here is a list of the things to look for; they appear again and again in the Slim Cuisine pudding and dessert recipes.

1 **Skimmed milk**. Widely available chilled, and in long-life boxes. It is very easy to switch your palate from full-fat milk to skimmed milk. For the first day or so, the skimmed version may seem a bit thin, but after a week – if you then try to go back to full-fat or part-skimmed products – you will find that the fat in the milk is disgustingly obtrusive: it coats the tongue in a revolting manner and – when added to coffee or tea – floats in horrible fatty globules on the surface. Give yourself a week to break the full-fat habit – it's easier than you think.

2 **Skimmed milk powder**. In experimenting with very low-fat dessert cookery, I found that augmenting skimmed milk with additional skimmed milk powder imparts a wonderful richness to ice creams, bread puddings, and other desserts where a perception of creaminess is important. To make it even more attractive, skimmed milk powder is fortified with vitamins A and D, two of the fat-soluble vitamins.

3 **Skimmed milk yoghurt**. Read the label. Many yoghurts – although labelled low-fat – are actually only *part*-skimmed. Buy yoghurts that contain less than 1% fat.

4 **Fromage frais**. As with yoghurt, read the label before buying. There are 0% fat, 20%, and 40% formulations of fromage frais available – buy the 0% only. The name – fromage frais (fresh cheese) – is misleading; the product is more like a superbly creamy, rich soured cream than cheese. Mixed with honey and vanilla it makes an incomparable creamy topping for scones and cakes (see page 81).

5 **Quark**. A *smooth* (unlike cottage cheese which has horrid little lumps) skimmed milk curd cheese that is absolutely marvellous when whipped with sugar or NutraSweet and flavourings, and then used in all sorts of interesting desserts. Cheesecakes made with quark, for instance, taste *nothing* like 'diet' cheesecakes, although that is exactly what they are. Some supermarkets sell their own brand of skimmed milk curd cheese, which can be used in any recipe that calls for quark.

6 **Cottage cheese**. Despite the lumps, this can be quite useful – in fact if you whirl it in the liquidizer, the lumps will vanish. As with all dairy products, *read the label* and buy only the cheese that contains less than 1% fat. If you cannot find quark, or other smooth skimmed milk curd cheeses, you may make an approximation with cottage cheese: put the cheese in the liquidizer and

blend, carefully pushing it down on to the blades with a rubber spatula, until it is very smooth, with no trace of graininess. Scrape the cheese into a sieve lined with damp cheesecloth, and set it over a bowl. Leave in the fridge to drain overnight. (Pour off the liquid in the bowl every once in a while. By the way – that liquid can be used for bread baking.)

7   **Buttermilk**. Real buttermilk is the liquid left over from making butter. It is fat-free, because all the butterfat has gone into the butter. The buttermilk that you buy in the store is not the real thing – it is a beautifully creamy cultured skimmed milk product. What a wonderful baking ingredient it is, and how valuable for making Slim Cuisine food processor ice creams. Commercial buttermilk can be frozen, *if* you have a serious freezer that will freeze it quickly. In fact I find that frozen and thawed buttermilk is creamier and thicker than buttermilk that has *not* been frozen and thawed. Some commercial buttermilk cartons carry the caveat: do not freeze. This is because when thawed, they become grainy if frozen slowly in an inferior freezer such as the little freezer compartments found in small refrigerators. I checked with a dairy that produces a nationally distributed brand of buttermilk, and they concur that there is no problem in freezing, if it is done in a freezer that freezes fast, and keeps it solidly frozen.

EGGS

Egg yolks are high in fat and cholesterol, but egg whites are virtually fat-free, and an excellent source of high-quality protein. Despite the fat, an egg is a nice package of nutrition. If you are on the Slim Cuisine weight *loss* plan, you should consume no egg yolks at all, but you may use as many whites as you please in your cookery. You should also avoid egg yolks if your blood cholesterol level is high. Again, in this case, you may use the egg whites without worry.

On the Slim Cuisine weight maintenance plan (for people with no blood cholesterol problems) an occasional whole egg – yolk and all – would be no problem, but current thinking suggests that it is not wise to go beyond three a week.

Calorie Note

This book, like my other Slim Cuisine books, is meant to help you 'beat the system'. With Slim Cuisine you can eat lavishly and deliciously without the heartbreaking overweight that usually follows. All the recipes in this book use no added fat: no butter,

18

oil, lard, suet, margarine, solid vegetable shortening, or any other type of pure fat. Whole eggs, with their fatty high-cholesterol yolks, have been kept to a minimum, and high-fat nuts are not used at all. Cream and any other full-fat or part-fat dairy products have been avoided as well. Producing gorgeous desserts *without* these traditional killer ingredients has been one of the most exhilarating challenges of my professional career. I feel that I have, indeed, beaten the system: I can have my cake (and my pie and ice cream and bread pudding . . .) and I can keep my slim figure too. Because the fat dimension is missing from these recipes, and the empty sugar Calories have been cut back, the Calorie levels of these puddings have been drastically reduced. Remember, fat weighs in at 120 Calories per tablespoon (more than twice the Calories, gram for gram, of carbohydrate or protein). What's more, fat is metabolized differently from carbohydrate and protein; it goes directly to the body's fat stores with heartbreaking efficiency. A very low-fat content means that you automatically save hundreds (sometimes thousands!) of the most fattening kind of Calories, therefore I have *not* included Calorie counts for each recipe. I believe that obsessive Calorie-counting is demoralizing and self-defeating. Eliminate the fat, keep the nutrient density high, and the Calories take care of themselves.

How to Use These Recipes

Note: all ingredients are given in imperial and in metric measurements. Use one or the other, but do not mix measurements in any one recipe.

Before attempting to make one of these desserts, follow this procedure:
1   Read the recipe all the way through.
2   Prepare all ingredients, and measure them out. Set the prepared ingredients out on your work table.
3   Set out any equipment needed.
Then proceed with the recipe.

Symbols Used in This Book

♡ A recipe flagged with a heart indicates that the recipe is suitable for the Slim Cuisine weight *loss* regime. Recipes without hearts are suitable for Slim Cuisine weight maintenance. Some recipes are followed by instructions for ♡ variations.

🕐 A recipe flagged with a clock indicates a recipe that can be prepared very quickly.

❄ A snowflaked recipe is suitable for freezing.

⊠ This symbol indicates that a microwave is needed to prepare the recipe.

A Dose of Nostalgia

'She sent for one of those short, plump little cakes called *petites madeleines* which look as though they had been moulded in the fluted scallop of the pilgrim's shell. And soon, mechanically, weary after a full day with the prospect of a depressing morrow, I raised to my lips a spoonful of the tea in which I had soaked a morsel of the cake . . . a shudder ran through my whole body, and I stopped, intent upon the extraordinary changes that were taking place. An exquisite pleasure invaded my senses.'

Marcel Proust, *Swann's Way*

Bread Pudding

Talk about nostalgia! Mention bread pudding to some folks, and they go all soft and dreamy. There is *nothing* quite like a good bread pudding. It's the voluptuous texture of the custard-soaked bread, baked – ideally – so that the pudding mysteriously combines lightness *and* stodginess in each sweet mouthful. I've seen recipes for 'lighter' bread puddings made with less bread, but with lots more eggy, creamy custard and lots more butter. Such formulas don't interest me: they cut back on the beautiful complex carbohydrate (bread) and pile on the fat. They don't taste quite right either. A good, nostalgic bread pudding should not levitate off the tongue like a soufflé. If you want a soufflé make one, for heaven's sake. A good bread pudding should linger for a moment or two – *then*, it should levitate. I've found that a glorious bread pud can be produced utilizing *no* fat at all, not even egg yolks. Each mouthful of these gorgeous puddings caresses the tongue like edible velvet, before sliding gently down in the most comforting way imaginable. I can hardly even write about it without wanting to rush madly into the kitchen to whip one up *at once*.

To ensure perfection in your bread puddings, follow these rules:

1   Use a good quality bakery bread that has been allowed to stand for a day or so, out of its wrapper.
2   After combining the bread with the custard, always allow it to stand for a few hours or overnight, so that the bread is thoroughly soaked with the custard mixture. Don't leave it to soak longer, or the pudding will be wet and soggy.
3   Always bake the bread pudding in a hot water bath: the pudding dish should rest in a larger, boiling-water-filled baking dish.
4   A bread pudding is a substantial dish – in fact, I always think that it is too substantial to be a dessert, unless it follows a truly stingy meal. Why not have a bread pudding as a meal in itself – breakfast, lunch, tea, light supper? In addition to tasting terrific, my bread puddings provide a lovely package of nutrients. They stand beautifully on their own.

For some people, bread puddings operate as a sort of edible time machine, propelling the pudding-eater back to an earlier, less complicated time of life. All I can say is: enjoy the trip!

BANANA BREAD PUDDING

Serves 4

I ask myself: how can something made from stale bread, skimmed milk and egg whites taste so outrageously good? The basic ingredients sound so austere, but – mixed with ripe bananas, rum and orange juice – they form an unforgettable bread pudding.

1 tablespoon rum	5fl oz/150 ml fresh orange juice
2–3 tablespoons raisins	5 egg whites
1 teaspoon natural vanilla essence	5 tablespoons light brown sugar
6 oz/175 g 1–2-day-old unsliced	16 fl oz/425 ml skimmed milk
bakery white bread	3 tablespoons skimmed milk powder
1lb/450 g ripe bananas, peeled and	
sliced	

1   Combine the rum, raisins and vanilla essence and let soak.
2   Cut the bread into ¾–1-inch/2–2.5-cm chunks. Put them in a 12 × 7-inch/30.5 × 18-cm, 2-inch/5-cm deep baking dish. Mix in the peeled, sliced bananas and orange juice.
3   Beat together the egg whites with the sugar. Gently beat in the milk, milk powder and rum–raisin mixture. Pour the mixture over the bread. Use a broad spatula to push the bread into the liquid. Stir it all up, but be careful not to break up the bread. Cover the dish and refrigerate for several hours (or overnight).
4   Remove the dish from the refrigerator, and let stand at room temperature while you preheat the oven to 350°F, 180°C, Gas Mark 4. Put the kettle on to boil.
5   Choose a baking dish larger than the one containing the bread. Put it in the preheated oven. Put the bread dish in the larger dish. Pour boiling water in the larger dish to come about half-way up the sides of the smaller dish. Bake for 30–40 minutes, until puffed and firm. (A knife inserted near the centre will emerge clean.)
6   Cool the bread pudding on a rack. Serve warm or at room temperature.

PINEAPPLE BREAD PUDDING

Serves 4

I love basic recipes like bread pudding. I think of them the way Mozart thought of simple tunes: what scope for variation! What a wonderful excuse for a positive orgy of creativity! Low-fat bread puddings are wonderful when dressed up with fresh, dried or tinned fruit (don't turn up your nose at tinned fruit; it is an excellent, versatile and convenient foodstuff) and liqueurs. This version, with crushed pineapple and a splash of dark rum, pleases both adults and children.

---

6 oz/175 g 1–2-day-old unsliced bakery white or brown bread
1 tin (15¼ oz/432 g) crushed pineapple in natural juice, with juices
5 egg whites
6 tablespoons light brown sugar

16 fl oz/425 ml skimmed milk
3 tablespoons skimmed milk powder
1 tablespoon dark rum
1 teaspoon natural vanilla essence
2–3 tablespoons raisins
Grated rind of ½ orange

---

1   Cut the bread into ¾–1-inch/2–2.5-cm chunks. Put them in a 12 × 7-inch/30.5 × 18-cm, 2-inch/5-cm deep baking dish together with the crushed pineapple and its juices.

2   Beat the egg whites with 5 tablespoons of the sugar. Gently beat in the milk and remaining ingredients except for the additional brown sugar. Pour the mixture over the bread. Use a broad spatula to push the bread into the liquid. Stir it all up, but be careful not to break up the bread. Sprinkle the remaining brown sugar evenly over the top. Cover the dish and refrigerate for several hours (or overnight).

3   Remove the dish from the refrigerator, and let stand at room temperature while you preheat the oven to 350°F, 180°C, Gas Mark 4. Put the kettle on to boil.

4   Choose a baking dish larger than the one containing the bread. Put it in the preheated oven. Put the bread dish in the larger dish. Pour boiling water in the larger dish to come about half-way up the sides of the smaller dish. Bake for 30–40 minutes, until puffed, browned and firm. (A knife inserted near the centre will emerge clean.)

5   Cool the bread pudding on a rack. Serve warm or at room temperature.

PEAR BREAD PUDDING

Serves 4

Tinned fruit is a blessing in the dead of winter. In this pudding, the pears take on a melting texture that plays beautifully against the custardy bread.

6 oz/175 g 1–2-day-old unsliced bakery white or brown bread	16 fl oz/425 ml skimmed milk
2 tins (14½ oz/411 g each) pears in natural juice, quartered	3 tablespoons skimmed milk powder
5 fl oz/150 ml juice from pears	1 tablespoon orange brandy
5 egg whites	1 teaspoon natural vanilla essence
6 tablespoons light brown sugar	2–3 tablespoons raisins
	Grated rind of ½ orange

1 Cut the bread into ¾–1-inch/2–2.5-cm chunks. Put them in a 12 × 7-inch/30.5 × 18-cm, 2-inch/5-cm deep baking dish, together with the quartered pears and the pear juice.

2 Beat the egg whites with 5 tablespoons of brown sugar. Gently beat in the milk and remaining ingredients except for the additional tablespoon of brown sugar. Pour the mixture over the bread. Use a broad spatula to push the bread into the liquid. Stir it all up, but be careful not to break up the bread. Sprinkle the remaining brown sugar evenly over the top. Cover the dish and refrigerate for several hours (or overnight).

3 Remove the dish from the refrigerator, and let stand at room temperature while you preheat the oven to 350°F, 180°C, Gas Mark 4. Put the kettle on to boil.

4 Choose a baking dish larger than the one containing the bread. Put it in the preheated oven. Put the bread dish in the larger dish. Pour boiling water in the larger dish to come about half-way up the sides of the smaller dish. Bake for 50–60 minutes, until puffed and firm. (A knife inserted near the centre will emerge clean.)

5 Cool the bread pudding on a rack. Serve warm or at room temperature.

PEAR–CHOCOLATE BREAD PUDDING

Serves 4–6

This is not an intensely chocolatey bread pudding (if you want intensity, see pages 94 and 124). The light chocolate presence complements the pears very well.

---

6 oz/175 g 1–2-day-old unsliced bakery white or brown bread
2 tins/14½ oz/411 g each) pears in natural juice, cubed
5 fl oz/150 ml juice from pears
5 egg whites
6 tablespoons brown sugar

16 fl oz/425 ml skimmed milk
3 tablespoons skimmed milk powder
1 tablespoon dark rum
1 teaspoon natural vanilla essence
3 rounded tablespoons low-fat unsweetened cocoa (see Mail Order Guide, page 133)

---

1   Cut the bread into ¾–1-inch/2–2.5-cm chunks. Put them in a 12 × 7-inch/30.5 × 18-cm, 2-inch/5-cm deep baking dish, together with the cubed pears and the pear juice.
2   Beat the egg whites with 5 tablespoons of brown sugar. Gently beat in the milk, milk powder, rum and vanilla. Sift in the cocoa, and whisk well to combine thoroughly. Pour the mixture over the bread. Use a broad spatula to push the bread into the liquid. Stir it all up, but be careful not to break up the bread. Sprinkle the remaining brown sugar evenly over the top. Cover the dish and refrigerate for several hours (or overnight).
3   Remove the dish from the refrigerator, and let stand at room temperature while you preheat the oven to 350°F, 180°C, Gas Mark 4. Put the kettle on to boil.
4   Choose a baking dish larger than the one containing the bread. Put it in the preheated oven. Put the bread dish in the larger dish. Pour boiling water in the larger dish to come about half-way up the sides of the smaller dish. Bake for 30–40 minutes, until puffed and firm. (A knife inserted near the centre will emerge clean.)
5   Cool the bread pudding on a rack. Serve warm or at room temperature.

Variation: Pear–Cherry–Chocolate Bread Pudding

As above, but use 1 tin (14½ oz/411 g) pears, cubed, and ½ lb/ 225g cherries, stoned and halved.

ORANGE–LYCHEE BREAD PUDDING

Serves 4–6

I would say that this is my all-time best bread pudding. As with all bread puddings in this collection, it would make a beautiful sweet meal on its own: breakfast, tea, light supper.

---

6 oz/175 g 1–2-day-old unsliced bakery white or brown bread
1 tin (15 oz/425 g) lychees in natural juice
1 tin (11 oz/295 g) mandarins in natural juice
4 fl oz/100 ml juice drained from the mandarins

1 tablespoon crystallized ginger, finely chopped (use scissors)
5 egg whites
5 tablespoons light brown sugar
16 fl oz/425 ml skimmed milk
3 tablespoons skimmed milk powder
1 teaspoon natural vanilla essence

---

1   Cut the bread into ¾–1-inch/2–2.5-cm chunks. Put them in a 12 × 7-inch/30.5 × 18-cm, 2-inch/5-cm deep baking dish, together with the drained lychees, the mandarins and 4 fl oz/ 100 ml of their juice, and the ginger.

2   Beat the egg whites with 4 tablespoons of brown sugar. Gently beat in the milk, milk powder and vanilla. Pour the mixture over the bread. Use a broad spatula to push the bread into the liquid. Stir it all up, but be careful not to break up the bread. Sprinkle the remaining brown sugar over the surface of the pudding. Cover the dish and refrigerate for several hours (or overnight).

3   Remove the dish from the refrigerator, and let stand at room temperature while you preheat the oven to 350°F, 180°C, Gas Mark 4. Put the kettle on to boil.

4   Choose a baking dish larger than the one containing the bread. Put it in the preheated oven. Put the bread dish in the larger dish. Pour boiling water in the larger dish to come about half-way up the sides of the smaller dish. Bake for 30–40 minutes, until puffed and firm. (A knife inserted near the centre will emerge clean.)

5   Cool the bread pudding on a rack. Serve warm or at room temperature.

BREAD PUDDING WITH CHERRIES

Serves 4–6

Once it was possible to buy pound bags of very good quality frozen cherries in freezer stores across the country. Should they be available in your local freezer store, you will be able to make this pudding all year round – not just when fresh cherries are in season. In that case, substitute the drained juices of the cherries for the orange juice, but add a bit of grated orange rind.

6 oz/175 g 1–2-day-old unsliced bakery white or brown bread	*1 teaspoon each: natural vanilla and almond essences*
5 egg whites	*Pinch or two of cinnamon*
3–4 tablespoons caster sugar	*(optional)*
16 fl oz/425 ml skimmed milk	*1 lb/450 g pitted cherries*
3 tablespoons skimmed milk powder	*4 fl oz/100 ml fresh orange juice*

1   Cut the bread into ¾–1-inch/2–2.5-cm chunks. Put them in a 12 × 7-inch/30.5 × 18-cm, 2-inch/5-cm deep baking dish.
2   Beat the egg whites with the sugar. Gently beat in the milk, milk powder and flavourings. Pour the mixture over the bread. Use a broad spatula to push the bread into the liquid. Add the cherries and the orange juice. Stir it all up, but be careful not to break up the bread. Cover the dish and refrigerate for several hours (or overnight).
3   Remove the dish from the refrigerator, and let stand at room temperature while you preheat the oven to 350°F, 180°C, Gas Mark 4. Put the kettle on to boil.
4   Choose a baking dish larger than the one containing the bread. Put it in the preheated oven. Put the bread dish in the larger dish. Pour boiling water in the larger dish to come about half-way up the sides of the small dish. Bake for 30–40 minutes, until puffed and firm. (A knife inserted near the centre will emerge clean.)
5   Cool the bread pudding on a rack. Serve warm or at room temperature.

FRENCH TOAST WITH PEACHES

Serves 4–6

My versions of French toast are simply variations of bread pudding. Here, slices of custard-soaked bread are topped with fresh fruit and baked in a flan tin. Traditionally, French toast is made by soaking slices of stale bread in an eggy custard and then *frying* the slices in butter. Baking the soaked slices results in a much more delicious dish: a sort of custardy bread and fruit tart. To serve, cut in wedges, like a pie. What a festive and happy breakfast it would make!

½ pint/300 ml peaches (diced over a measuring jug)	6–7 oz/175–200 g thinly sliced stale white or brown bakery bread
2 fl oz/50 ml orange juice	3 egg whites
2 fl oz/50 ml Amaretto liqueur	8 fl oz/225 ml skimmed milk
4 tablespoons light brown soft sugar	2 tablespoons skimmed milk powder
	1 teaspoon natural vanilla essence

1 Combine the peaches, juice, liqueur, and 1 tablespoon of sugar. Let macerate for 15–30 minutes.
2 Arrange the slices of bread so that they cover the bottom of an 11–12-inch/28–30.5-cm non-stick flan tin. Cut the bread into halves and quarters if necessary.
3 Pour the peaches and their juices evenly over the bread.
4 Beat the egg whites with the remaining sugar. Gently beat in the remaining ingredients. Pour evenly over the bread and peaches. Cover and refrigerate for several hours, or over-night.
5 Preheat the oven to 350°F, 180°C, Gas Mark 4. Bring the bread and peaches to room temperature. Bake in a boiling water bath for 35–45 minutes, until puffed and done (a knife inserted near the centre will emerge clean). Serve at once, or cool on a rack. Great for breakfast, tea, or as a dessert.

CINNAMON–ALMOND FRENCH TOAST

Serves 4

Here we have slices of stale baguette, soaked in cinnamon-and almond-flavoured custard, and baked until the bread is creamy textured within, and crispy on top. Perfect for breakfast or tea. Because this contains 3 whole eggs, it is not for those with high blood cholesterol levels. For people with no such problem, the occasional whole egg will do no harm.

6 oz/175 g stale baguette, sliced ¾ inch/1.5-cm thick	16 fl oz/425 ml skimmed milk
3 eggs	½ teaspoon each: natural vanilla essence, natural almond essence, ground cinnamon
2 egg whites	
3½–4 tablespoons caster sugar	

1   Arrange the slices of bread in overlapping rows so that they cover the bottom of a 12 × 7-inch/30.5 × 18-cm, 2-inch/5-cm deep baking dish.
2   Beat the eggs and whites with the sugar. Gently beat in the remaining ingredients. Pour evenly over the bread. With a broad spatula, push the bread into the liquid. Cover and refrigerate for several hours, or overnight.
3   Preheat the oven to 350°F, 180°C, Gas Mark 4. Bring the bread mixture to room temperature. Bake in a boiling water bath for 35–45 minutes, until puffed and done. Serve at once, or cool on a rack.

RICE PUDDING

Makes approximately 2 pints/1.1 litres

In my old fat days I used to make rice pudding with loads of egg yolks, butter and double cream. When I became slim I was determined to develop a very low-fat version, but I wanted no part of a rice pudding that is anaemic, thin and dietetic. How wonderful to report total success. This rice pudding is rich in the tastes and textures of caramelized milk and sugar, and creamy rice. The procedure couldn't be simpler: stir the ingredients together and bake in a hot water bath – that's all. You *do* have to stir it every 20–30 minutes, but that's not a difficult task, merely tedious. Tedium pays, however – I'll wager that this is one of the best rice puddings ever to soothe your soul.

6 tablespoons raisins or sultanas	6 rounded tablespoons skimmed milk powder
6 tablespoons Amaretto liqueur	1 vanilla bean
1 oz/25 g caster sugar	4 oz/110 g pudding rice
2 pints/1.1 litres skimmed milk, at room temperature	

1   Combine the raisins and liqueur in a small bowl and let soak while you preheat the oven to 300°F, 150°C, Gas Mark 2.
2   Thoroughly stir together the sugar, milk, and milk powder. Split the vanilla bean lengthwise with a paring knife. With the tip of the knife, scrape out the interior of the bean. Scrape this black, aromatic material into the milk and stir to thoroughly mix it in. (Save the scraped pod for vanilla sugar or vanilla NutraSweet, see page 16.) Stir in the rice, and the raisins with their liqueur.
3   Pour this mixture into a 9-inch/23-cm square, 2-inch/5-cm deep baking dish. Place the baking dish in a larger baking dish and pour boiling water into the larger baking dish, so it comes two-thirds of the way up the sides. Bake for approximately 2¼ hours, stirring after each 20–30-minute period. It is done when the rice is tender, and bathed in a thick, creamy sauce. It will not be *too* soupy, but on the other hand the liquid should not be completely absorbed. Serve warm or cold.

⊕ ⊠ Rice Pudding: Microwave Version

Makes approximately 2 pints/1.1 litres

Use of the microwave reduces the 2 plus hours of baking to a paltry 30 minutes or so. Even so, you must stir, stir, stir. This is just as creamy as the conventional version, but the cooking time is too short for the caramelized milk–sugar flavour to develop. Still, it is quite marvellous.

6 tablespoons raisins or sultanas	*6 rounded tablespoons skimmed*
6 tablespoons Amaretto liqueur	*milk powder*
1 oz/25 g caster sugar	*1 vanilla bean*
2 pints/1.1 litres skimmed milk, at	*4 ozs/110 g pudding rice*
room temperature	

1   Combine the raisins and liqueur in a small bowl and let soak.
2   Thoroughly stir together the sugar, milk, and milk powder. Split the vanilla bean lengthwise with a paring knife. With the tip of the knife, scrape out the interior of the bean. Scrape this black, aromatic material into the milk and stir to thoroughly mix it in. (Save the scraped pod for vanilla sugar or vanilla NutraSweet, see page 16.) Stir in the rice, and the raisins with their liqueur.
3   Pour this mixture into a 9-inch/23-cm square, 2-inch/5-cm deep baking dish. Place the baking dish in the microwave,

Chocoholics unite: clockwise from lower left: chocolate-almond pie; chocolate roulade filled with banana cream; chocolate icecream, chocolate sorbet, and a truly remarkable chocolate pudding.

The soup is *supposed* to be cold! Bottom: raspberry-peach soup with peach sorbet; left: blueberry soup with blueberry sorbet; right: hot and cold pineapple.

and microwave on full power for 35 minutes, stopping the machine to stir the mixture thoroughly every 5 minutes. It is ready when the rice is *al dente* (tender but with a slight 'bite') and bathed in a creamy sauce. When done, let stand for 10 minutes, stirring occasionally.

> All recipes in this collection that call for a microwave were tested with a 700-watt machine. You will need to adjust the timing of the recipes to match the idiosyncrasies of your particular machine. Always jot down the cooking time after trying a recipe out for the first time – then there will be no need to guess next time.

' . . . *a rice cream, like air-filled pebbles in the mouth* . . . '
Molly Keene, *Nursery Cooking*

♡ ⊕ ⊠ BLAMELESS RICE PUDDING

Makes 1¼ pints/700 ml

Not only does this rice pudding contain no fat, it also contains no sugar. And – as with the previous microwave variation – the tedium of preparation has been reduced; use of the microwave cuts the preparation time by a third. Lemon peel flavours the pudding, but you may substitute orange peel or a touch of almond essence extract (or more cinnamon) if you wish. This pudding fits into the Slim Cuisine weight-*loss* plan, but is it creamy? Is it comforting? Is it delicious? You bet it is!

4 oz/110 g pudding rice	1 teaspoon natural vanilla essence
2 pints/1.1 litres skimmed milk, at room temperature	2 cartons (14 oz/400 g) quark
6 tablespoons skimmed milk powder	4 tablespoons granulated NutraSweet
½ teaspoon ground cinnamon	½ lemon

1 Thoroughly stir together the rice, milk, milk powder, cinnamon and vanilla essence in a 9 inch/23cm square, 2 inch/5cm deep baking dish suitable for the microwave.
2 Microwave at full power for 35 minutes, stopping the machine to stir the mixture thoroughly every 4–5 minutes. It is ready when the rice is *al dente* (tender but with a slight 'bite') and bathed in a creamy sauce. When done, let stand for 5 minutes, stirring occasionally.

3   While the rice is standing, combine the quark and NutraSweet in the processor container. Finely zest ¼–½ of the lemon rind right over the processor container so that the zest goes in (see box) and some of the lemon oil as well. Process until the quark is smooth and fluffy.
4   With a rubber spatula, fold together the quark and creamy rice. Serve at once.

Zesting Note

To zest a lemon, use a zester, an inexpensive little gadget that neatly removes fine slivers of zest from the citrus fruit. If you wield the zester right over the bowl containing the rest of the recipe's ingredients, then some of the aromatic lemon oil will go in along with the slivers of zest. This is important: zest lightly – the zest itself is lovely, the white pith beneath the zest is strong and bitter. If you dig in too strenuously, the finished recipe may have an underlying bitter flavour. Another important point: always scrub citrus fruit before zesting, to remove any wax or traces of insecticide.

⊕ SWEET NOODLE PUDDING

Makes approximately 3 pints/1.7 litres (this recipe can easily be halved, or even quartered)

In Eastern Europe, sweet noodle desserts are legion. They come in all sorts of guises: baked, fried, grilled, or – at their simplest – boiled and tossed into a sweet buttery and creamy sauce. I have had no luck in producing a decent Slim Cuisine version of a baked or fried noodle pudding, but boiled and tossed – that's another story. If you boil up some broad noodles, dump them, hot and steaming, into fragrant vanilla- and orange-flavoured curd cheese, throw in a few plump raisins and sultanas, and toss the whole kaboodle together until each tender noodle is bathed in the aromatic, creamy sauce . . . There is not a collywobble, a bluefunk or a mubblefubble in the known universe that can withstand such bliss.

3 tablespoons raisins	3–4 tablespoons skimmed milk
3 tablespoons sultanas	1 teaspoon natural vanilla essence
2 tablespoons water	3 rounded tablespoons soft light
2 tablespoons orange liqueur	brown sugar
(Cointreau or Grand Marnier)	1 lb/450 g broad noodles, such as
2 large oranges	tagliatelle
1 large lemon	Additional soft light brown sugar
28 oz/800 g quark	Ground cinnamon

1   Combine the raisins, sultanas, water and orange liqueur in a small saucepan. Add the juice from both oranges and the slivered zest from ½ orange and ½ lemon. Simmer until the raisins are plump and the liquid has reduced to 1–2 tablespoons. Set aside.

2   Put the quark, milk, vanilla and sugar in the food processor container. Zest another ½ orange and the remaining ½ lemon right over the container, so that the zest goes in and some of the aromatic oils as well. Process until very smooth and creamy. Set aside.

3   Warm a large bowl. Cook the noodles according to the package directions. When they are tender (but not mushy), drain well, then dump into the warm bowl. With 2 large spoons, toss them with the raisins and their juices. Pour and scrape in the creamy mixture. Toss and turn with the 2 spoons until the noodles are thoroughly coated with the sauce.

4   Serve at *once* in deep, warm bowls. Provide a dessertspoon and fork for each diner. Have a shaker of cinnamon and a sugar basin of soft light brown sugar on the table. Each person can shake on cinnamon and sprinkle on sugar to their taste.

'No matter where they come from or where they've ended up, Hungarians of all ages love noodles. Given a good túrós metélt [noodles with curd cheese], a Hungarian far from home will surely kiss the cook's hand, for these are the dishes that mother used to make.'
Susan Derecskey, *The Hungarian Cookbook*

PASSOVER MATZOH CARROT CHARLOTTE

One of the dietary restrictions of the Jewish Passover is the elimination of all forms of leaven and of grain. Only matzoh is allowed, an unleavened cracker-like wafer that has been baked under strict religious supervision. Every year, Jewish cooks exhibit considerable ingenuity turning out flourless cakes and desserts. Passover recipes are usually beloved family heirlooms, turning up year after year, generation after generation, and always greeted with deep affection. This charlotte is a recipe I've used for years at Passover – I 'Slim-Cuisined' it when I gave up fat.

*½ Granny Smith apple, peeled and
grated*
2 tablespoons lemon juice
3 oz/90 g sugar
5 fl oz/150 ml grated carrots
*2 fl oz/50 ml cream sherry or sweet
Kosher dinner wine*
*6 tablespoons medium motzah meal
(available all year round in many
supermarkets)*

6 egg whites, at room temperature
Pinch cream of tartar
*½ teaspoon cinnamon (or
½ teaspoon natural vanilla
essence, or almond essence, or
natural coconut extract)*

1   Preheat oven to 375°F, 190°C, Gas Mark 5.
2   Toss together the grated apple, lemon juice, half the sugar, the grated carrots, sherry and motzah meal.
3   In an impeccably clean bowl, with an impeccably clean beater, beat the egg whites on medium speed until foamy. Add the cream of tartar, and beat at higher speed until they hold soft peaks. Beat in the remaining sugar, a little at a time, until it is dissolved and the egg whites hold firm peaks.
4   Stir 2 big spoonfuls of the egg whites into the carrot batter, to lighten it.
5   With a rubber spatula, fold the remaining egg whites into the carrot mixture. Sprinkle on the cinnamon, and fold it in. Pile the mixture into a shallow baking dish. Bake until golden, and a thin skewer tests clean – about 35 minutes. Serve at once.

'On the table, the fresh crisp matzos were also waiting, and . . . such wonderful chremzlach [sweet matzo meal fritters] that it would have been hard even for an epicure to tell if there was more honey in them or more chicken fat because they were so sugary and rich that they stuck to the gums, and ran down his beard.'
Sholom Aleichem, *The Lottery Ticket*

Be Fruitful

'I opened the door of the old refrigerator; it was not empty
. . . it was heaped with fruit, shelves swelled with it,
every color, every texture, and hidden within, every kind
of pit. There were greengage plums, black plums, red
plums, apricots, nectarines, peaches, long horns of
grapes, black, yellow, red, and cherries, cherries flowing
out of boxes and staining everything scarlet. And there
were melons – cantaloupes and honeydews, on the top
shelf, half of a huge water-melon, a thin sheet of wax
paper clinging to its bare red face like a wet lip. Oh
Patimkin! Fruit grew in their refrigerator and sporting
goods dropped from their trees!'

Philip Roth, *Goodbye Columbus*

Can She Bake a Cherry Pie?

Old-fashioned open fruit pies: apple, cherry, peach, blueberry . . . the mouth waters, the heart sings. Unfortunately, no-fat, no-oil pie doughs make great cardboard. Believe me, I've attempted to beat many, many versions of no-fat pie crusts into submission, to no avail. Sideways thinking (I was determined to have my apple pie, no matter how many times my pie crusts hardened into rigor mortis) brought to mind the French clafouti – a tender, puffy, fruit-filled open pancake. Clafoutis responded to my no-fat and low-fat experiments with the utmost good nature. I worked out several versions of fruit flans based on the clafouti method. They may be prepared with no fat at all, or with just one egg yolk, otherwise no additional fat. And they may be prepared with white or brown flour. Each, in its own way, is quite glorious. In preparing these flans, use a trusty, no-fail, *non-stick* fluted flan tin, or – for the rectangular cake versions – a porcelain or ceramic baking dish. Cool thoroughly before serving. To serve, use a triangular pie server. Cut a wedge or a square, then gently and carefully slide the pie server right under the wedge or square, separating it from the side and bottom of the dish. Carefully lever it up, and put it on a plate. If you wish, pour some fruit coulis over each serving.

These flans deserve the best fresh fruit available. Use them to celebrate the bounty of the season.

CHERRY–PEACH FLAN

Makes 1 10-inch/25-cm flan

This is wonderful. *No* egg yolks (therefore *no* fat). A tender pastry crust forms on the bottom, fluffy custard on top. Amazing! See page 42 for the variations possible.

24 fl oz/670 ml peaches and cherries (see recipe)	2 teaspoons natural vanilla essence
3 tablespoons sugar	2 tablespoons sugar
⅕ pint/100 ml orange juice	Pinch salt
8 fl oz/225 ml skimmed milk	2½ oz/60 g self raising sponge flour
4 tablespoons skimmed milk powder	Pinch nutmeg
	5 egg whites

1   Preheat oven to 350°F, 180°C, Gas Mark 4.
2   Pit the peaches and cut into wedges over a measuring jug to catch their juices. Halve and pit the cherries over the jug. You need 24 fl oz/670 ml in all. Combine the fruit with the sugar and orange juice.
3   Combine the milk, powdered milk, vanilla essence, sugar, salt, flour, nutmeg and egg whites in the liquidizer jar. Process until very well blended. Let sit for 30 minutes.
4   Pour 5 fl oz/150 ml of the batter into an 11–12-inch/28–30.5-cm non-stick pie tin. Bake for 4 minutes. Top with the prepared fruit and juices. Pour the remaining batter over the fruit. Bake for 50–60 minutes, until golden brown and puffed. (Put a flat baking sheet on the bottom of the oven to catch any drips.) Cool thoroughly on a rack. (It will subside somewhat.) Serve at room temperature.

'I made a pie last night.'
'A pie.' Marcia looked at him for a minute and then she said, 'Apple?'
David shook his head and she said, 'Pineapple' and he shook his head again and because he could not wait to tell her, said, 'Cherry.'
'My God!' . . . She watched happily while he cut large pieces . . . and then she tasted the pie and made wordless gestures of appreciation.'
Shirley Jackson, *Like Mother Used to Make*

APRICOT–CHERRY FLAN

Makes 1 10-inch/25-cm flan

Here is an equally wonderful (but quite different) one-yolk, brown-flour version: in the finished flan, the fruit is surrounded by the tender dough.

24 fl oz/670 ml apricots and cherries (see recipe)	2 teaspoons natural vanilla essence
3 tablespoons sugar	2 tablespoons sugar
⅕ pint/100 ml orange juice	Pinch salt
4 fl oz/100 ml skimmed milk	2½ oz/60 g self-raising brown flour
4 fl oz/100 ml buttermilk	Pinch nutmeg
4 tablespoons skimmed milk powder	3 egg whites
	1 whole egg

1   Preheat oven to 350°F, 180°C, Gas Mark 4.
2   Pit the apricots over a measuring jug and cut into wedges. Halve and pit the cherries over the jug. You need 24 fl oz/670 ml in all. Combine the fruit with the sugar and orange juice.
3   Combine the milk, buttermilk, powdered milk, vanilla essence, sugar, salt, flour, nutmeg, egg whites and whole egg in the liquidizer jar. Process until very well blended. Let sit for 30 minutes.
4   Pour 5 fl oz/150 ml of the batter into an 11–12-inch/28–30.5-cm non-stick pie tin. Bake for 4 minutes. Top with the prepared fruit and juices. Pour the remaining batter over the fruit. Bake for 50–60 minutes, until golden brown and puffed. (Put a flat baking sheet on the bottom of the oven to catch the drips.) Cool thoroughly on a rack. (It will subside somewhat.) Serve at room temperature.

APPLE–RAISIN FLAN

This is the white-flour version of the one-yolk fruit flan; the dough has a bit more delicacy than the brown-flour version.

1 lb/450 g Granny Smith apples, peeled, cored and cut into wedges	4 tablespoons skimmed milk powder
3 tablespoons raisins	2 teaspoons natural vanilla essence
Slivered zest of ½ orange and 1 lemon	2 tablespoons sugar
2 fl oz/50 ml orange juice	Pinch salt
1 fl oz/25 ml lemon juice	2½ oz/60 g white self-raising flour
1 fl oz dark rum	Pinch each: cinnamon, nutmeg, and mace
4 fl oz/100 ml skimmed milk	3 egg whites
4 fl oz/100 ml buttermilk	1 whole egg

1   Preheat oven to 350°F, 180°C, Gas Mark 4.
2   Combine the apples, raisins, grated orange and lemon zest, orange juice, lemon juice and rum.
3   Combine the milk, buttermilk, powdered milk, vanilla essence,

sugar, salt, white flour, cinnamon, nutmeg, mace, egg whites and whole egg in the liquidizer jar. Process until very well blended. Let sit for 30 minutes.

4   Pour 5 fl oz/150 ml of the batter into an 11–12-inch/28–30.5-cm non-stick pie tin. Bake for 4 minutes. Top with the prepared fruit and juices. Pour the remaining batter over the fruit. Bake for 50–60 minutes, until golden brown and puffed. (Put a flat baking sheet on the bottom of the oven to catch the drips.) Cool thoroughly on a rack. (It will subside somewhat.) Serve at room temperature.

Variations on Fruit Flans: The possibilities are infinite; this list only scratches the surface. It represents combinations that my assistant and I have tried, but I'm sure that you will find your own favourites. Let the seasonal array of fruit at the greengrocer be your inspiration.

Pear–Raspberry Flan: using 4 pears, 1 punnet raspberries, 2 fl oz/ 50 ml orange liqueur, 2 fl oz/50 ml orange juice.
Melon–Strawberry Flan: using a mixture of 24 fl oz/670 ml fruit, ⅕ pint/100 ml orange juice.
Melon–Nectarine: using a mixture of 24 fl oz/670 ml fruit, ⅕ pint/ 100 ml orange juice.
Melon–Peach: using a mixture of 24 fl oz/670 ml fruit, ½ pint/300 ml orange juice.
Blueberry–Cherry: using a mixture of 24 fl oz/670 ml fruit, ⅕ pint/ 100 ml orange juice.

BLUEBERRY CAKE

This variation of the one-yolk, white-flour clafouti batter (with porridge oats added) makes a wonderfully tender, berry-filled cake. To serve, cut into squares and, using a triangular pie server, carefully separate the bottom of the square from the dish, then lever the square out.

1 lb 6 oz/625 g blueberries, rinsed, drained and picked over	2½ oz/60 g self-raising sponge flour
3 tablespoons caster sugar	3 egg whites
Slivered zest of ½ large orange	1 whole egg
6 fl oz/175 ml fresh orange juice	8 fl oz/225 ml skimmed milk
Pinch salt	3 tablespoons caster sugar
	4 tablespoons porridge oats

1   Preheat oven to 375°F, 180°C, Gas Mark 4.
2   Combine the berries, 3 tablespoons sugar, orange zest, juice and salt in a shallow 12½ × 8½-inch/31.5 × 21.5-cm non-reactive baking dish (porcelain or pottery works best).
3   Combine all the remaining ingredients in the container of the liquidizer. Blend very well. Add the oats. Flick the liquidizer on and off a few times to blend thoroughly. Let stand for 30 minutes.
4   Stir up the batter and pour it evenly over the berries. Bake for 40–50 minutes, until done. The blueberry juices will be bubbling up through the batter, and it may crack a bit, but that's fine. A skewer or toothpick will test clean. Let stand on a rack until *completely* cooled. (It's best the next day.) Cut into squares and serve right from the pan.

PEACH CAKE

This is gorgeous – a *very* crumbly cake with lots of peaches. Really, it is peaches encased in a bare minimum of wholemeal, one-yolk clafouti batter. To serve, cut in squares and *gently* ease each square up with a pie server.

7–8 ripe peaches, pitted and diced (dice over a bowl to catch their juices)	Pinch salt
	2½ oz/60 g wholewheat self-raising flour
3 tablespoons caster sugar	3 egg whites
Slivered zest of ½ large orange	1 whole egg
6 fl oz/175 ml fresh orange juice	8 fl oz/225 ml skimmed milk
	3 tablespoons caster sugar

1   Preheat oven to 375°F, 180°C, Gas Mark 4.
2   Combine the peaches, their juices, 3 tablespoons sugar, the orange rind, orange juice and salt in a shallow 12½ × 8½-inch/31.5 × 21.5-cm non-reactive baking dish (porcelain or pottery works best).
3   Combine all the remaining ingredients in the container of the liquidizer. Blend very well. Let stand for 30 minutes.
4   Stir up the batter and pour it evenly over the peaches. Bake for 40–50 minutes until done. A skewer or toothpick will test clean. Let stand on a rack until *completely* cooled. (It's best the next day.) Cut into squares and serve right from the pan.

'Talking of pleasure, this moment I was writing with one hand and with the other holding to my mouth a Nectarine – good God, how fine

It went down soft, pulpy, slushy, oozy – all its delicious embonpoint *melted down my throat like a large, beatified strawberry.'*
John Keats, in a letter

RED AND BLUE FRUIT CAKE

This version of the rectangular clafouti one-yolk batter cake has three sections: red (cherries), blue (blueberries), and red again (raspberries). Cut and serve as described in the previous recipes.

10 oz/275 g stoned, halved cherries	*2½ oz/60 g self-raising sponge*
10 oz/275 g raspberries	*flour*
10 oz/275 g blueberries	*3 egg whites*
3 tablespoons caster sugar	*1 whole egg*
6 fl oz/150 ml orange juice	*8 fl oz/225 ml skimmed milk*
Pinch salt	*3 tablespoons caster sugar*

1　Preheat oven to 375°F, 180°C, Gas Mark 4.
2　Divide the fruit into 3 separate parts in a shallow, rectang-ular 12½ × 8½-inch/31.5 × 21.5-cm non-reactive baking dish (porcelain or pottery works best). Combine the sugar, orange juice and salt and pour over the fruit.
3　Combine all the remaining ingredients in the container of the liquidizer. Blend very well. Let stand for 30 minutes.
4　Stir up the batter and pour evenly over the fruit. Bake for 40–50 minutes until done. A skewer or toothpick will test clean. Let stand on a rack until *completely* cooled. (It's best the next day.) Cut into squares and serve right from the pan.

FRUIT PIZZA

Makes 2 crusts (one can be frozen for another time)

This 'pizza' is simply an attractive fruit tart: a baked crust spread with several fruit compôtes.

1 lb/450 g self-raising sponge flour	*2 tablespoons runny honey*
Pinch salt	*3–4 fruit compôtes of your choice*
½–1 pint/300–570 ml buttermilk	*(see page 73)*

1   Preheat the oven to 400°F, 200°C, Gas Mark 6.
2   Put the flour into a large bowl. Sprinkle the salt over it. Make a well in the middle of the flour.
3   Pour ½ pint/300 ml buttermilk into the well. With a wooden spoon, stir the flour into the buttermilk. Add the honey and more buttermilk as needed to form a rather rough, slightly sticky dough. Switch from the spoon to both hands, and knead for a few turns. Don't overwork it, or it will be tough.
4   Divide the dough into two. Stretch and pat each half to fit a non-stick 11-inch/28-cm flan tin. Press each half into a tin, and press against the tin to flute the edges.
5   Bake blind (see note) for 20 minutes. Remove weights and paper. Bake for an additional 10–15 minutes. Remove from the oven and cool on a rack. Freeze one crust if desired.
6   When cooled, spoon 3–4 different fruit compôtes in neat sections over the crust.

Note: To bake blind, put a sheet of greaseproof paper into the dough-lined dish, and weight with dried beans. After baking, save the beans in a covered jar to re-use whenever you need to bake blind again.

♡ NO-SUGAR, NO-COOK SUMMER PUDDING

Serves 4

When I left America for England, six years ago, my friends saw me off with dire warnings. 'You'll hate it,' they assured me. 'Everyone knows that the English have no tastebuds. You won't last a month!' Oh, how wrong they were. I've been on a six-year odyssey of gastronomic discovery: shepherd's pie, Yorkshire pudding, steamed samphire, gooseberry fool . . . But the most stunning discovery of all has been summer pudding. Who ever heard of such a thing in the US of A? Certainly not me. Certainly not my gourmet pals. Who would have guessed that you could take some old bread, some ripe berries, a pudding basin, and put them together in such a glorious way? Here is my version, developed over the past few years for those who *love* the pudding, but *hate* the flab.

7–8 thin slices bakery white bread, 1–2 days old	and stoned and halved or quartered red cherries
1¾ lb/800 g mixed red fruit: halved strawberries, whole raspberries	Granulated NutraSweet to taste 1 punnet strawberries

1 Trim the crusts from the bread, and cut, diagonally, into quarters. Use some of them to line the bottom and sides of a 2-pint/1.1-litre pudding basin. Cut or tear small pieces of bread to patch any spaces.

2 Put the mixed red fruits in a bowl and crush with a potato masher until the juices run. Sweeten to taste, and crush and mash a bit more. Pour the fruit and juices into the bread-lined basin. Use the remaining bread pieces to cover the fruit, leaving no spaces. Choose a saucer or plate that fits in the basin, and place it on top of the pudding. Put a tin on the plate to weight it. (If possible remove a shelf from the fridge so there is plenty of headroom.) Put the pudding in the fridge, place a cutting board over the tin on the saucer, and put two more big tins on the board. Leave for *at least* 8 hours.

3 Remove the weights and plate. Loosen the sides of the pudding with a palette knife. Turn out on to a plate.

4 Hull and halve the remaining punnet of strawberries. In a bowl, mash and crush with a potato masher until the juices run. Sweeten to taste with NutraSweet. Use this sauce to paint over any mottled patches on the pudding. Surround the pudding with the remaining sauce and serve.

WINTER PUDDING

Serves 4

When berries are out of season and you don't have any frozen ones to hand, try substituting a compôte of diced, dried fruits for the red fruit in the summer pudding recipe. 'Luscious' is the word that comes to mind to describe it. The bread soaks up the syrupy compôte juices: the texture of the juice-soaked bread against the chewy/tender texture of the fruit pieces, coupled with the sweet/ tart balance of flavours, make this pudding outstanding.

Dried Fruit Compôte

4 tablespoons sultanas
1 lb/450 g mixed dried fruit
   (apricots, apples, figs, prunes,
   pears), diced, as if for mincemeat
8 fl oz/225 ml dry white wine

1½ oz/40 g caster sugar
½ cinnamon stick
Juice and grated zest of 1 lemon
4–6 fl oz/100–175 ml fresh orange
   juice

1   Combine the sultanas, dried fruit, 8 fl oz/225 ml water, and the wine in a baking dish. Allow to soak for 1 hour.
2   Preheat the oven to 350°F, 180°C, Gas Mark 4.
3   At the end of the hour, stir in the sugar, cinnamon stick, and lemon juice and zest. Cover the dish and bake for 1 hour. Cool and refrigerate until needed (it keeps for weeks).
4   When the compôte has thoroughly cooled, stir in the fresh orange juice.
5   Line a pudding basin with bread as for summer pudding (see page 45), substituting the fruit compôte for the red fruits. Cover the fruit with bread, weight and refrigerate for at *least* 8 hours.
6   When you turn the pudding out on to a plate, paint over any pale bits with orange juice.

⊕ FRUIT SOUFFLÉ

Serves 3–4

In the dead of winter, pull out a tin of fruit, whip up a few egg whites, and – in 15 minutes – you have a gossamer, fruit-imbued soufflé that almost floats right out of its dish.

1 tin (14-15 oz/400-425 g) fruit in natural juice (pears, apricots or peaches)	3 egg whites, at room temperature
	Pinch salt and cream of tartar
	1–2 tablespoons sugar
1 tablespoon orange liqueur (Cointreau or Grand Marnier)	

1   Preheat oven to 400°F, 200°C, Gas Mark 6.
2   Drain the fruit and mash with a potato masher to a rough purée. Stir in the liqueur.
3   Beat the egg whites in an electric mixer on medium speed until foamy. Add the salt and cream of tartar and beat on highest speed, adding the sugar a little at a time, until the sugar is dissolved and the whites are shiny and thick and hold firm peaks.
4   Stir a tablespoon of meringue into the fruit purée. Fold in the remainder. Spoon the mixture into a 2-pint/1.1 litre soufflé dish. Bake for 15 minutes, or until beautifully puffed and golden.

❄ MAREN'S FRUIT DUMPLINGS

Makes approximately 9 dumplings

My friend Maren Mauder sent me her family recipe for old-fashioned fruit dumplings. Originally these dumplings were fattening: Maren 'Slim-Cuisined' them with great success. As with most sweetly comforting dishes, this goes far beyond dessert. It would make a wonderful light supper. Sweet dreams would surely follow.

9 oz/250 g quark	3 tablespoons semolina
1 whole egg	3 tablespoons fine natural
Pinch salt	breadcrumbs
3 tablespoons self-raising flour	5 plums, halved and pitted

1   Mix together all the ingredients except the plums to make a pliable dough.
2   Take part of the dough and roll into a thick sausage. Cut into thick slices and flatten somewhat.
3   Put a plum half on to each slice. Press down and mould the dough around the fruit to make a ball. Flour your hands if the dough tends to stick. Repeat with the remainder of the dough. (This freezes well. To freeze, immediately place the dumpling on a baking sheet in the freezer. When all are on the tray, cover with cling film. When solidly frozen, remove from the tray and place in plastic bags.)
4   Steam unfrozen dumplings over boiling water for approximately 15–18 minutes, frozen ones for approximately 20 minutes.
5   Serve with very low-fat fromage frais and caster sugar or Honeyed Vanilla Cream (page 81).

♡ ❄ *No-Yolk Variation*: Use 2 egg whites in place of 1 whole egg. After making a pliable dough, allow to rest in the refrigerator for 30 minutes before continuing. Serve with fromage frais and NutraSweet.

PEAR–SWEET POTATO MERINGUE

Serves 4–6

Sweet potatoes and pears – a marriage made in heaven. Layer them in a gratin dish, brush with honey and orange juice, dust with cinnamon, and bake under a blanket of apricot-and-vanilla-scented meringue. This is comfort food at its finest.

4 pears, thinly sliced	½ tablespoon runny honey
2 sweet potatoes, thinly sliced	2 teaspoons water
1 tablespoon runny honey	1–2 pinches cinnamon
5 fl oz/150 ml orange juice	

Topping

2 egg whites, at room temperature	2 teaspoons orange liqueur
Pinch of cream of tartar	1 teaspoon natural vanilla essence
1–1½ tablespoons sugar	1 tablespoon no-sugar apricot fruit spread

1 Preheat the oven to 400°F, 200°C, Gas Mark 6.
2 Overlap alternating thin slices of pear and sweet potato in an oblong or rectangular glass dish 12 × 7½ inches/30.5 × 18.5-cm.
3 Stir together the 1 tablespoon of honey with the orange juice and pour over the pears and potatoes.
4 Mix together the remaining ½ tablespoon of honey with the water and cinnamon and use it to brush over the pears and potatoes as they bake.
5 Bake for approximately 45–60 minutes, until tender (but not mushy) and caramelized.
6 With an electric mixer, beat the egg whites until they are foamy. Add the cream of tartar and beat until the whites hold firm peaks, adding the sugar, liqueur, vanilla and fruit spread as you beat.
7 Spread the meringue topping over the pear and sweet potato base and bake for a further 10 minutes until golden. Serve hot or warm.

APPLE–RAISIN MERINGUE

Serves 4–6

An apple–raisin version of the previous pear–sweet potato meringue. I leave the apples unpeeled, because I like the leathery texture of the baked apple skins, but you can peel them if you prefer.

4 tart eating apples, in wedges	2 pinches cinnamon
4 tablespoons raisins	1 pinch nutmeg
1 tablespoon honey	½ teaspoon honey
4 fl oz/100 ml orange juice	2 teaspoons water
Slivered zest of 1 lemon	

Topping

2 egg whites, at room temperature	1 teaspoon natural vanilla essence
Pinch cream of tartar	1 tablespoon no-sugar apricot fruit
1–1½ tablespoons sugar	spread
2 teaspoons calvados, brandy, or dark rum	

1   Preheat the oven to 400°F, 200°C, Gas Mark 6.
2   Overlap the wedges of apple in an oblong glass dish 12 × 7½ inches/30.5 × 18.5-cm. Sprinkle the raisins over the apples.
3   Mix together the 1 tablespoon of honey, orange juice, lemon zest, cinnamon and nutmeg and pour over the apples and raisins.
4   Combine the remaining honey and water and use to brush over the apples and raisins as they bake.
5   Bake in the oven for 15–20 minutes, until the apples are *just* tender, but not mushy. Flash under the grill to caramelize a bit if necessary.
6   With an electric mixer, beat the egg whites until they are foamy. Add the cream of tartar and beat until the whites hold firm peaks, adding the sugar, calvados, vanilla and fruit spread as you beat.
7   Spread the meringue topping over the apples and bake for a further 10 minutes until golden. Serve hot or warm.

✳ BANANA ROULADE

Serves 4–6

To make a banana roulade, an airy banana–egg white soufflé-like batter is baked flat, cooled, filled with Banana Cream or Chestnut-Orange Cream and rolled. When it is sliced, I love the way the smooth, soothing cream filling oozes out of the spongy spirals of the slices.

---

3 very ripe bananas	*Approximately 2 tablespoons of*
1 tablespoon dark rum	*sugar (less if the bananas are*
½ teaspoon nutmeg	*very sweet)*
½ teaspoon cinnamon	*½ teaspoon natural vanilla essence*
1 scant tablespoon lemon juice	*2 oz/50 g self-raising sponge flour,*
8 egg whites, at room temperature	*sifted*
Pinch of cream of tartar	*Icing sugar*

Filling: Banana Cream (page 52) or Chestnut-Orange Cream (page 73)

---

1   Line a non-stick baking sheet (13 × 9 inches/33 × 23-cm) with silicone baking paper. Set aside.
2   Preheat the oven to 350°F, 180°C, Gas Mark 4.
3   Cut the bananas into thick slices. Purée with the rum, the spices and the lemon juice in a food processor or blender. Scrape into a large bowl.
4   Beat the egg whites in an electric mixer on medium speed until foamy. Add the cream of tartar and beat on highest speed, adding the sugar a little at a time, until the sugar is dissolved and the whites are shiny and thick and hold firm peaks. Fold in the vanilla.
5   Gently fold the whites into the banana mixture, together with the sifted flour.
6   Gently spoon and spread all the banana mixture on to the prepared baking sheet. It will seem like an enormous amount, but don't worry. After it bakes and cools, it collapses somewhat. Bake for 20–30 minutes (a toothpick should test clean). Cool the pan on a rack.
7   Spread a clean tea towel on your work surface. Cover with a sheet of waxed or greaseproof paper. Sprinkle lightly and evenly with icing sugar. When thoroughly cooled, turn the roulade base out on to the paper, then peel off the silicone paper.
8   Spread the base with filling. Starting with a long edge, roll the base like a Swiss roll. Use the tea towel to help you roll it.

It may crack a bit, but it doesn't matter. Chill until needed. Serve in slices, with 'whipped' cream (page 99) if desired.

⊕ GRILLED BANANAS AND RUM

Serves 3–4

Versions of bananas sautéed in butter and flamed in rum occur in several cuisines. This version *bakes* them in orange juice and a touch of rum and brown sugar, with the same delectably rich result. To shock and delight the senses, try serving each portion of the bananas piping hot with a scoop of cold creamy Banana–Ginger Sorbet on top.

---

3 very ripe bananas	*1 tablespoon dark rum*
Juice of ½ lime and ½ lemon	*1 heaped tablespoon brown sugar*
3 fl oz/90 ml fresh orange juice	

---

1   Preheat the grill to its highest setting.
2   Peel the bananas, cut in half lengthwise, then cut each half in half, crosswise.
3   Put the citrus juices and rum in a shallow baking dish that can hold the banana pieces in one layer. Turn the bananas in the juice. Arrange, cut sides down, in one layer, and sprinkle evenly with sugar.
4   Grill 3 inches/8-cm from the heat for 3–5 minutes, or until the bananas are well browned on top.
5   Tilt the dish and drain the juices into a small saucepan or frying pan. Boil the juices briefly to thicken them.
6   Pour the juices back over the bananas. Top each hot serving with a dollop of Banana Cream (below), Honeyed Vanilla Cream (page 81), or Banana–Ginger Sorbet (page 107).

♡ Omit Sugar. Serve with Banana Cream or Banana–Ginger Sorbet.

♡ BANANA CREAM

Makes 1½ pints/900 ml

I love bananas for their versatility as well as for their sweet taste and luscious texture. Grilled in their skins, then beaten into fromage frais, they make a banana cream that has a gratifying *fattening* taste to it. The cream can be piped through a bag into dessert goblets. Or use it as a mousse in *coeur à la crème* moulds (see below), as a creamy topping for fruits, berries or Banana–Chocolate Torte, or as a filling in the Chocolate Roulade (see page 126).

---

4 grilled bananas, and their juices (see below)	2 tablespoons thawed orange juice concentrate
28 oz/800 g quark or very low-fat curd cheese (4 small cartons)	1 teaspoon natural vanilla essence
	½ teaspoon ground cinnamon
	NutraSweet to taste

---

1   Spoon the bananas out of their skins. Put them, with their juices, into the processor container along with the quark, orange juice concentrate, vanilla and cinnamon. Process until very smooth and fluffy. Taste. Process in some NutraSweet and a bit more cinnamon if needed.
2   Chill for several hours or overnight, so that the flavour develops and the mousse 'sets'. If some liquid separates out on to the top of the mousse, pour it off.

♡ ⊕ GRILLED BANANAS IN THEIR JACKETS

Grilled bananas originally appeared in *The Slim Cuisine Diet*; they are too good not to repeat here. Grilling a banana intensifies its natural sweetness, and turns it into a banana-custard within its skin. This has to be one of the easiest (and sweetest!) of puddings. Grilled bananas also feature as a star ingredient in several recipes.

---

1   Preheat the grill. Line the grill tray with foil, shiny side up. Place the rack on the grill tray. Choose very ripe bananas and put these, *unpeeled*, on the grill rack. Grill, about 1 inch/2.5-cm from the heat, for approximately 3 minutes on each side, until the bananas have swelled up, are speckled with charred bits, and are spitting and spluttering like mad.
2   With tongs, carefully transfer the bananas to a plate. Peel a strip off the top of each. Pour the juices from the grill tray on to the bananas. Eat with a spoon.

Coeur à la Crème

Coeur à la crème moulds are small, pierced, white porcelain heart-shaped moulds. They are available in many cookware shops (or see Mail Order Guide page 133). *Coeurs à la crème* are made by lining the moulds with muslin that has been rinsed in cold water and wrung out, then spooning a creamy mixture into the lined moulds. The overhanging muslin is flipped over to cover the mixture, and the moulds are set on a plate to drain in the refrigerator for several hours or overnight. At serving time, coat a small plate with a fruit coulis, unwrap the mould, and flip the drained, heart-shaped creamy mixture on to the coulis. Garnish with berries or mint leaves if you wish. Banana Cream (page 52), Strawberry Cream (below), or any of the cheesecake fillings (pages 114–119) would make splendid *coeurs à la crème*. Large moulds are available as well if you prefer to make one large one instead of individual servings.

♡ ❄ STRAWBERRY CREAM

Strawberry Cream (like Banana Cream on page 52) can be served piped into goblets, or wrapped in muslin and drained overnight in *coeur à la crème* moulds. Be very fussy and buy the best strawberries when they are in season. Sniff before you buy – proper berries should have a powerful strawberry fragrance.

---

2 punnets very ripe strawberries, hulled and halved	*1 teaspoon natural vanilla essence*
	NutraSweet to taste
28 oz/800 g quark (4 small cartons)	*Fresh strawberries and mint leaves*
1 tablespoon thawed orange juice concentrate	*for garnish*

---

1   Put the strawberries in a shallow bowl. Mash them with a potato masher until you have a lumpy, juicy purée.
2   Put the quark, the strawberries and their juices, orange concentrate and vanilla in the processor container, and process for a moment or so. Taste and add NutraSweet as needed. Process until fluffy. Drain for an hour or so in a cheesecloth-lined sieve set over a bowl.

⊕ CHERRIES IN STRAWBERRY SAUCE

Serves 4

When the cherry and strawberry season is in full swing, it is such pleasure to just eat them as they are, in great quantities, until your lips and fingers are stained with their red juices. But there *is* a limit – the time comes when you want to eat them in a manner that is a bit more formal then simply gobbling them by the handful.

2 punnets over-ripe strawberries	*½ pint/300 ml fromage frais*
1 tablespoon soft brown sugar	*Meringue cookies (optional) (see*
1½ lb/720 g fresh cherries	*page 80)*

1   Hull the strawberries, put them in a bowl and sprinkle with half the sugar. Mash roughly with a potato masher until their juices begin to run and you have a lumpy purée. Set aside.
2   Stem and pip the cherries. Divide them between 4 stemmed goblets.
3   Fold the fromage frais into the strawberry purée. Spoon this mixture over the cherries. Sprinkle a bit of the remaining sugar over the top of each serving and place a meringue in each goblet. Serve at once.

♡ Substitute NutraSweet for the sugar; omit the meringue.

REDCURRANT–PLUM SAUCE

Makes ½–¾ pint/300–400 ml

Redcurrants can take a lot of sweetening, so I suggest using a combination of sugar and NutraSweet for the best flavour with the fewest empty Calories. This sauce is very good on toasted slices of Angel Cake (page 60).

1½ pints/900 ml mixed redcurrants	*2 tablespoons cornflour*
and chunked, unpeeled red plums	*1 tablespoon orange juice*
4 tablespoons sugar	*1 tablespoon vanilla NutraSweet or*
Pinch salt	*to taste (see page 16)*

1   Combine fruit, sugar, salt, cornflour and orange juice in a saucepan. Simmer until tender and thick.
2   Sieve the fruit mixture and then add vanilla NutraSweet to taste.

Have Your Cake

'I rarely saw him – between meals mind you – without a large chunk of cake heavily coated with sugar icing in his hand.'

Alice Laden, *The George Bernard Shaw Vegetarian Cookbook*

Angel Cake

Making a cake without a speck of fat and oil is easy. In fact one of the most classic cakes of all, the Angel Cake, is made exactly that way – no egg yolks, no butter, no oil, no shortening of any sort, not even a smear to grease the tin. A successful Angel Cake is tender and airy, and fun to make: with no other cake do you get to hang it upside down on a bottle to cool. Your first Angel Cake will probably terrify you: when the time comes to actually turn the thing – tin and all – upside down and jam it on to the neck of a bottle, you will feel sure that disaster is imminent. Don't worry. Because the straight sides of the Angel Cake tin remain ungreased, the soufflé-like batter is able to cling to the sides and rise to majestic height. When you suspend the finished cake upside down it will not slip out to squash itself silly on the counter.

The rules for making Angel Cake are similar to the rules for making soufflé:

1   You will need to separate the yolks and whites of several eggs. Years ago a friend with no cooking experience tried to bake a cake. The recipe said, 'separate 3 eggs'. She took one egg and put it on the kitchen counter, put another egg on the table and the third on the cooker. They were well separated, but she couldn't figure out what to do next. I had to explain that separating meant separate the *whites* from the *yolks*. Cold eggs separate easier than room-temperature ones, but room-temperature egg whites whip up to a greater volume than chilled ones. As a result it's best to separate the yolks from the whites while the eggs are cold, then allow the whites to reach room temperature before whipping them.
2   Always make sure that every speck of yolk is gone from the white, and that your bowl and beater are impeccably clean. Even a speck of grease will prevent the whites from whipping into a cloud of meringue.
3   A pinch of cream of tartar (available from most supermarkets) adds a bit of acidity and enables the egg whites to whip to their maximum volume.

A few words about Angel Cake tins. A classic Angel Cake should be made in an Angel Cake tin: a tube tin with a removable bottom. (See Mail Order Guide, page 133.) To use the tin, place the tube and bottom *inside* the tin. Angel Cakes are meant to be cooled upside down. When cooling the cake, carefully invert the tin over a bottle or inverted funnel. The neck of the bottle or funnel should come right through the tube. After the cake has cooled – at least an hour, preferably more – loosen it around the sides with a palette knife. Let it slide out on to a serving plate, then loosen the tube-bottom piece with a palette knife and lift it off.

ANGEL CAKE

Makes 1 10-inch/25.5-cm cake

4 oz/110 g self-raising sponge flour	*Pinch of cream of tartar*
3½ oz/85g caster sugar	*5½ oz/160 g caster sugar*
10 egg whites, at room temperature	*1½ teaspoons natural vanilla essence*

1   Preheat the oven to 375°F, 190°C, Gas Mark 5.
2   Sift together the flour and the 3½ oz/85 g sugar.
3   Beat the egg whites until foamy. Add the cream of tartar and beat until they hold soft peaks. Continue beating, adding the remaining 5½ oz/160 g sugar, 2 tablespoons at a time, until the sugar is dissolved, and the whites are stiff and glossy. Fold in the vanilla.
4   A little at a time, sprinkle the sifted flour/sugar mixture over the batter and fold in gently but thoroughly.
5   Gently spoon and push the meringue into an ungreased 10-inch/25-cm, 3½–4 inch/8.5–10-cm deep Angel Cake tin. Bake for 30–35 minutes. When it is done the top will most likely have cracked like a soufflé. The cake will spring back when gently pressed with your finger, and a cake tester will test clean.
6   Cool *upside down* by inverting the cake – in its tin – on a bottle (the neck of the bottle should come right up through the hole), or on an inverted funnel. Leave for at least 1 hour.
7   Use a long palette knife to loosen the cake gently along the sides and bottom of the pan, and around the tube. Gently shake, and slide out on to a plate. To serve, cut gently, using a sawing motion, with a long, sharp, serrated knife.

Variation: Dusky Angel Cake

Makes 1 10-inch/25.5-cm cake

It never hurts to add some chocolate, now – does it?

1　Reduce the amount of flour to 3 oz/75 g.
2　In Step 2, sift in 6 tablespoons unsweetened low-fat cocoa with the sugar and flour.

BLACK AND WHITE ANGEL

Makes 1 10-inch/25.5-cm cake

The best of both worlds – an Angel Cake that is half vanilla, and half chocolate.

3 oz/75 g self-raising sponge flour	*10 egg whites, at room temperature*
9 oz/250 g caster sugar	*Pinch of cream of tartar*
3 tablespoons low-fat unsweetened	*1½ teaspoons natural vanilla*
cocoa powder	*essence*

1　Preheat the oven to 375°F, 190°C, Gas Mark 5.
2　Sift together 2 oz/50 g flour with 1½ oz/40 g sugar. Set aside.
3　Sift together 1 oz/25 g flour, 3 tablespoons cocoa powder and 2 oz/50 g sugar. Set aside.
4　Beat the egg whites with the cream of tartar until they hold soft peaks. Beat in 5½ oz/160 g sugar, 2 tablespoons at a time, until the sugar is dissolved and the whites are stiff and glossy and hold firm peaks. Fold in the vanilla.
5　Divide the mixture in half. Into one half fold in the white flour/sugar mixture; into the other half, fold in the cocoa/flour mixture.
6　Gently spoon and push the white batter into the ungreased Angel Cake tin. Spoon and push the chocolate batter evenly over the white. Bake for 30–35 minutes. (It is done when it springs back when gently poked with your finger, and a cake tester tests clean.)
7　Cool *upside down* by inverting it on a bottle (the neck of the bottle should come right up through the hole) or on an inverted funnel. Leave for *at least* 1 hour.
8　Use a long palette knife to loosen the cake gently along the sides and bottom of the pan, and around the tube. Gently shake, and slide out on to a plate. To serve, cut gently, using a sawing motion, with a long, sharp, serrated knife.

Angel Cake Suggestion: Slices of Angel Cake are absolutely splendid toasted. Top the toasted cake with fruit compôte, a scoop of ice cream, Hot Fudge Sauce, fresh berries and fromage frais – whatever pleases you.

The Inconsistency of Ovens

Before tackling any of the cake or flan recipes in this book (or tackling *any* oven-baked dish for that matter), stop for a moment and consider your oven. An oven is not an oven is not an oven. Several things affect its performance: is it fan-assisted? Is it small or large? Electric or gas? Is its thermostat working properly? Are you baking one thing alone, or several at a time? All these things affect the cooking time of a recipe. Learn to know your oven. Because ovens differ so, you must take the baking times listed in any recipe as an approximation. If a recipe suggests 15 minutes, your oven may need as little as 10 or as much as 20. Always use your first time out with a recipe as a test drive – note the cooking time needed, so you do not need to guess next time around. It is also important to note that most ovens are uneven. During baking, it is a good idea to turn cake tins, or if more than one thing is baking, switch their position, half-way through.

Stir Crazy

When my son was nine years old, his class went on an overnight camping trip (if I remember correctly, they set up their tents in the teacher's back garden). The unit they were studying was the American Pioneers, and the purpose of the overnight adventure was to let the children have a go at experiencing those tough Pioneers' ingenuity and self-sufficiency. Each child was to bring food: they were assigned to bring either something to cook on the fire, or a dessert personally made with the child's own hands.

Of course, when Shawm remembered to tell me that he was supposed to prepare and bring a dessert, it was just about an hour before he was due at the camp. And – of course – my larder happened to be particularly bare: no eggs, no milk . . . Now had Shawm expected me to whip up a Pioneer costume from a few odd scraps, I would have thrown a gasket, but culinary emergencies were just my cup of tea. After a moment's thought, I knew what to do: it was obviously time for me and my child to whip up a Stir Crazy cake. The Stir Crazy is an old recipe – it had been circulating around money-raising community charity cookbooks for generations. The recipe had fallen out of fashion, but – as a keen collector of culinary folklore – I knew all about it. The vague belief was that the Stir Crazy originated in the American Southwest, as part of the chuck wagon cuisine of the American cowboy, but I instinctively knew that theory to be hogwash. Its true source was obviously an anonymous but ingenious and weary mother who was faced with the same classic situation facing me at that moment – the pressing need for a large, child-pleasing dessert, that had to be rapidly conjured out of the most basic ingredients. The original Stir Crazy recipe went something like this: pull out a cake pan – don't grease it. Dump some flour, sugar and cocoa powder *right into the pan*. Dump in some cooking oil, white vinegar (for its leavening power) and vanilla essence. Pour some water over the whole thing, grab an old wooden spoon, stir it all up *right in the pan*, shove it into the oven, and, in approximately 20 minutes – *voilà*! (or the Early American equivalent) – a chocolate cake! Obviously, a child could make this cake. Well, my child did, and served it at the camp to great acclaim – in fact at the end of the year his teacher ended her written yearly report on Shawm with this comment: 'I'll never forget that chocolate cake!'

I never forgot it either, and while pondering, recently, the nature of cake batters, and their dependence on fats, I thought I'd have a go at the good old Stir Crazy *without* the oil. My assistant and I stirred like crazy through experiment after experiment and – finally – came up with some beauties. To make a basic Slim Cuisine Stir Crazy you dump self-raising sponge flour, sugar and low-fat cocoa powder into a non-stick flan tin, dump vanilla, water and buttermilk over them, and stir. Sprinkle on some white vinegar (it helps leaven the cake, but you will not taste it in the finished cake), stir again and bake. In 15 minutes you have a flattish, rich, fudgy cake that tastes very much like that other American chocolate classic – the brownie. Why not serve wedges of Stir Crazy topped with scoops of Chocolate Sorbet or Chocolate Ice Cream? Why not add a sluice of Strawberry or Raspberry Coulis? And how about a scattering of fresh raspberries in season? Oh, how I *love* my work!

⚓ STIR CRAZY FUDGY CHOCOLATE TORTE

Makes 1 10-inch/25.5-cm torte

The secret of a good Slim Cuisine Stir Crazy is: *do not overcook it!* When done, it will be set but not at all dry – the texture will be fudgy and slightly wet.

5½ oz/160 g self-raising sponge flour	Pinch salt
	1 teaspoon natural vanilla essence
6 oz/175 g caster sugar	4 fl oz/100 ml water
1 oz/25 g low-fat unsweetened cocoa powder (see Mail Order Guide, page 133)	8 fl oz/200 ml thick buttermilk
	1 tablespoon white vinegar

1. Preheat the oven to 350°F, 180°C, Gas Mark 4.
2. Sift together the flour, sugar, cocoa and salt directly into a 10–11-inch/25–28-cm non-stick flan tin. Combine the vanilla, water, and buttermilk and pour the mixture over the dry ingredients in the pan.
3. With a wooden spoon, stir the mixture together in the pan, using a gentle circular motion. Stir gently but thoroughly, so that the dry ingredients are thoroughly incorporated into the liquid ones. Sprinkle on the vinegar, and gently stir it in.
4. Bake for approximately 15 minutes, until *just* done. It will be set, and the surface will spring back when lightly pressed. Cool on a rack. Serve warm or at room temperature.

⊕ STIR CRAZY BANANA–FUDGE TORTE

Makes 1 10-inch/25.5-cm torte

The addition of mashed ripe banana to the basic Stir Crazy turned out to be a very good idea. It can be served with a dollop of Banana Cream, or a scoop of Banana Ice Cream. Or how about a scoop of Banana Ice Cream and a nice puddle of Chocolate Sauce?

5½ oz/160 g self-raising sponge flour	1 tablespoon white vinegar
	1 teaspoon natural vanilla essence
4 oz/110 g caster sugar	
1 oz/25 g low-fat unsweetened cocoa powder (see Mail Order Guide, page 133)	4 fl oz/100 ml buttermilk
	4 fl oz/100 ml water
Pinch salt	2 **very** ripe bananas, peeled and mashed to a pulp

1. Preheat the oven to 350°F, 180°C, Gas Mark 4.
2. Sift the flour, sugar, cocoa and salt directly into a 10–11-inch/25–28-cm non-stick flan tin. Combine the vinegar, vanilla, buttermilk and water and pour the mixture over the dry ingredients in the pan. Add the bananas.
3. With a wooden spoon, stir the mixture together right in the

Be a Soda Jerk in your spare time: clockwise from bottom: banana split; chocolate shake; vanilla shake; mango rickey; raspberry rickey; hot fudge sundae.

Tea time: clockwise from top: reverse chocolate chip cookies; chocolate meringues; chocolate-almond chewies with strawberry cream; apple-sultana buns; fudgy chocolate-banana torte with banana cream; redcurrant-plum sauce.

Morning coffee: clockwise from upper right: blueberry compôte; French toast with peaches; blueberry cake; peach cake; cherry cake; bagels with quark.

Life's little aggravations are soothed by frequent doses of cheesecake:
from right to left: pumpkin cheesecake; pineapple cheesecake.

pan, using a gentle circular motion. Stir gently but thoroughly, so that the dry ingredients are thoroughly incorporated into the liquid ones. The mixture will be lumpy from the banana pulp, but that's fine.

4   Bake for approximately 15 minutes until *just* done; it will be set, and the surface will spring back when lightly pressed. If it is allowed to overcook, it will be too dry; it must retain a fudgy texture.

5   Cool on a rack. Serve in wedges, warm or at room temperature. If you wish, garnish each serving with a piped dollop of Banana Cream (page 52).

STIR CRAZY CHOCOLATE AND RASPBERRY TORTE

Makes 1 13-inch/33-cm torte

The chocolate Stir Crazy batter makes an inspired base for raspberries. When fresh raspberries are in season, stir the batter in a bowl and spread it in a flan tin, sprinkle the berries over the batter, and bake until the batter is set but not at all dry. The bordering dough will spring back when lightly pressed; the centre will be, although set, still fudgy and not too firm. The baking time depends on the kind of pan you choose and – of course – on your particular oven (see box, page 62).

5½ oz/160 g self-raising sponge flour	1 teaspoon natural vanilla essence
6 oz/175 g caster sugar	4 fl oz/100 ml water
1 oz/25 g low-fat unsweetened cocoa	8 fl oz/200 ml thick buttermilk
powder (see Mail Order Guide,	1 tablespoon white vinegar
page 133)	2 pints/1.1 litres fresh raspberries
Pinch salt	2 tablespoons sugar

1   Preheat the oven to 350°F, 180°C, Gas Mark 4.

2   Sift together the flour, sugar, cocoa and salt into a bowl. In a jug, combine the vanilla, water, buttermilk and vinegar. Pour the liquid mixture over the dry ingredients in the bowl. With a wooden spoon, stir the mixture together using a gentle circular motion. Stir gently but thoroughly, so that the dry ingredients are thoroughly incorporated into the liquid ones.

3   Pour and scrape the batter into a 13-inch/33-cm flan dish. With a rubber spatula, spread it evenly over the dish.

4   Combine the raspberries and sugar and pour and scatter the mixture in one even layer over the chocolate batter, leaving a ½-inch/1-cm border all around.

5   Bake for approximately 50–60 minutes if using a metal flan tin – approximately 35 minutes for a china quiche dish (see box). The edges of the torte will be set, and the surface, when pressed around the rim, will spring back. The raspberry centre will remain somewhat wet, but will firm up as the torte cools.

Stir Crazy fruit tortes bake perfectly in a 13-inch/33-cm diameter, 1–1½-inch/2.5–3.5-cm deep fluted china quiche or flan dish. I bought two at the Royal Worcester factory outlet, and use them again and again to turn out splendid tortes. Stir Crazy fruit tortes may also be baked in 13-inch/ 33-cm diameter metal fluted flan tins (available in many house-ware shops), with or without removable bottoms. The cooking time for the china dish is quite a bit less (approximately 30 minutes in all) than the cooking time for the metal one (approximately 50 minutes in all). Exact timing depends on your particular oven. First time out with these recipes, check carefully, then note the minutes for next time. If you use the metal flan tin with the removable bottom, cool the torte thoroughly, then carefully loosen all around the sides, before slipping the torte out of the tin.

STIR CRAZY BLUEBERRY TORTE

Makes 1 13-inch/33-cm torte

This Stir Crazy (like the one that follows) has no chocolate in the batter. Blueberry pie is one of the great classics of American dessert cuisine. Remember the line in the song Nellie Forbush sings in *South Pacific*? 'I'm as corny as Kansas in August, I'm as normal as blueberry pie.' Take this recipe as my Slim Cuisine version of the old classic. It may not be 'normal', but it is as deliciously blueberryish as all get out.

Batter

6 oz/175 g self-raising sponge flour
3½ oz/85 g sugar
Pinch salt
1 teaspoon natural vanilla essence

4 fl oz/100 ml water
8 fl oz/225 ml buttermilk
1 tablespoon white vinegar

Fruit Mix

2 pints/1.1 litres blueberries
2 tablespoons sugar

Pinch salt
Slivered zest of ½ orange and
  ½ lemon

1   Preheat the oven to 350°F, 180°C, Gas Mark 4.
2   Sift together the flour, sugar and salt into a bowl. Combine the remaining batter ingredients in a jug, and pour over the flour. With a wooden spoon, gently stir the ingredients together, using a steady, circular motion. When the wet and dry ingredients are thoroughly amalgamated, pour and scrape the batter into a 13-inch/33-cm diameter flan dish. With a rubber spatula, evenly smooth the batter over the dish.
3   Combine together the fruit mix ingredients and pour and scatter the mixture in an even layer over the top of the batter, leaving a ½–1-inch/1–2.5cm border.
4   Bake in the oven for approximately 50–60 minutes if using a metal flan dish – approximately 35 minutes for a china one (see box, page 66). The edges of the torte will be set, and the surface, when pressed around the rim, will spring back. The blueberry centre will remain somewhat wet, but will firm up as the torte cools.

Variations: Use 2 pints/1.1 litres mixed raspberries, nectarines and strawberries, with 2–3 tablespoons sugar for the fruit mix.

Use 2 pints/1.1 litres mixed raspberries, peaches and cherries, with 3 tablespoons sugar for the fruit mix.

STIR CRAZY DRIED FRUIT TORTE

This Christmas, why not serve a Stir Crazy that overflows with succulent Slim Cuisine mincemeat in place of those wicked little mincemeat tarts? For Christmas you might want to make it a little boozier by substituting sherry and brandy for the dry white wine.

Dried Fruit Compôte

4 tablespoons sultanas
1 lb/450 g mixed dried fruit
  (apricots, apples, figs, prunes,
  pears), diced as for mincemeat
8 fl oz/225 ml water

8 fl oz/225 ml dry white wine
1 tablespoon caster sugar
½ cinnamon stick
Grated zest of ½ lemon

1   Combine the sultanas, diced fruit, water, and wine in a baking dish. Allow to soak for 1 hour.
2   Preheat the oven to 350°F, 180°C, Gas Mark 4.
3   At the end of the hour, stir in the sugar, cinnamon stick, and lemon zest. Cover the dish and bake for 1 hour. Refrigerate until needed (it keeps for weeks).

Batter

6 oz/175 g self-raising sponge flour
3½ oz/85 g sugar
Pinch salt
1 teaspoon natural vanilla essence

4 fl oz/100 ml water
8 fl oz/225 ml buttermilk
1 tablespoon white vinegar

1   Preheat the oven to 350°F, 180°C, Gas Mark 4.
2   Sift the flour, sugar and salt into a bowl. Combine the remaining batter ingredients in a jug. Pour over the flour. With a wooden spoon, gently stir the ingredients together, using a steady, circular motion. When the dry and wet ingredients are thoroughly amalgamated, pour and scrape the batter into a 13-inch/33-cm flan dish. With a rubber spatula, evenly smooth the batter over the dish.
3   Pour and scatter the Dried Fruit Compôte in an even layer over the top of the batter, leaving a ½-inch/1-cm border.
4   Bake in the oven for approximately 40 minutes if using a china dish, approximately 50 minutes for a metal one (see box, page 66). The torte will be set, and the surface, when pressed around the rim, will spring back.

Morning Coffee, Afternoon Tea

'The tea consumed was the very best, the coffee the very blackest, the cream the very thickest, there was dry toast and buttered toast, muffins and crumpets, hot bread and cold bread, white bread and brown bread, homemade bread and bakers' bread, wheaten bread and oaten bread; and if there be other breads than these they were there . . . '

Anthony Trollope, *The Warden*

Chestnut Creams

My friend Sally Rettig sent me a letter about a low-fat dessert she had concocted:

'Dear Sue,

I've been throwing together a lot of low-fat stuff for the people in my house of late and have been a bit desperate for puds. I just did this from the store-cupboard and they loved it. Pure invention, so it might need fiddling around with.
I whizzed a can of unsweetened chestnut purée in the processor and blended it with 0% fromage frais, some NutraSweet and a couple of spoons of instant coffee powder. Absolute raves all round. The Noel purée makes a paler, slightly blander version than the Faugier (this subtly tells you that it went down so well I had to do it twice). I swirled some fromage frais through it to make it real purty. Over to you, lady!

Lots of love
Sally.'

Her idea really got me going. One of the versions I subsequently tried involved cocoa. My secretary, who can detect the presence of chocolate before she even comes into the house, took it away to try out on her family; she reported that they all loved it spread on their breakfast toast. What a remarkable idea! If you wondered what low-fat treat you could substitute for peanut butter or hazelnut chocolate spread, here are several for you to clutch joyfully to your bosom (or – I should say – spread joyfully on your toast). In the heat of enthusiastic experimentation, my assistant and I came up with almond, vanilla and orange versions as well as Sally's coffee and my chocolate. I suspect you will think of some gorgeous variations of your own as well. After several mornings of happily eating these on toast, it struck me that the spreads were uncannily like buttercream. My assistant, Sandie (who has much better handwriting than I), spooned the mixture into a pastry bag and wrote 'Happy Birthday' and other clever things all over a large sheet of greaseproof paper. Eureka! Slim Cuisine icing. We made rosettes, curlicues, squiggles – oh, they were beautiful. So here is your buttercream substitute. It has that fabulous buttery creamy texture that rolls so delightfully over your tongue, and it tastes just fine. Use it to ice and decorate cakes (Angel Cakes, Chocolate Torte, Stir Crazy Tortes), to fill roulades, or to gladden your morning toast. Thanks Sally!

♡ ⊕ ❄ CHESTNUT–COFFEE CREAM

Yields ¾ pint/400 ml

---

8 oz/225 g unsweetened chestnut purée
9 oz/250 g fromage frais
1 teaspoon natural vanilla essence

1½ tablespoons NutraSweet (or to taste)
1½ teaspoons coffee granules

---

1 Place all the ingredients in the bowl of a food processor. Process until thoroughly blended.
2 Scrape into a muslin-lined sieve, set over a bowl. Refrigerate overnight to drain.

♡ ⊕ ❄ CHESTNUT–CHOCOLATE CREAM

Yields ¾ pint/400 ml

---

8 oz/225 g unsweetened chestnut purée
9 oz/250 g fromage frais
3 tablespoons NutraSweet (or to taste)

1 teaspoon natural vanilla essence
4 teaspoons low-fat, unsweetened cocoa powder (see Mail Order Guide, page 133)

---

1 Place all the ingredients in the bowl of a food processor. Process until thoroughly blended.
2 Scrape into a muslin-lined sieve set over a bowl. Refrigerate overnight to drain.

♡ ⊕ ❄ CHESTNUT–VANILLA CREAM

Yields ¾ pint/400 ml

---

8 oz/225 g unsweetened chestnut purée
9 oz/250 g fromage frais

1 teaspoon natural vanilla essence
1½–2 tablespoons NutraSweet (or to taste)

---

1 Place all the ingredients in the bowl of a food processor. Process until thoroughly blended.
2 Scrape into a muslin-lined sieve set over a bowl. Refrigerate overnight to drain.

♡ ⊕ ❋ CHESTNUT–ALMOND CREAM

Yields ¾ pint/400 ml

8 oz/225 g unsweetened chestnut purée	½ teaspoon natural almond essence
9 oz/250 g fromage frais	1–1½ tablespoons NutraSweet (or to taste)

1 Place all the ingredients in the bowl of a food processor. Process until thoroughly blended.
2 Scrape into a muslin-lined sieve set over a bowl. Refrigerate overnight to drain.

♡ ⊕ ❋ CHESTNUT–ORANGE CREAM

Yields ¾ pint/400 ml

8 oz/225 g unsweetened chestnut purée	3 tablespoons orange juice concentrate
9 oz/250 g fromage frais	1½–2 tablespoons NutraSweet
1 teaspoon natural vanilla essence	(or to taste)

1 Place all the ingredients in the bowl of a food processor. Process until thoroughly blended.
2 Scrape into a muslin-lined sieve set over a bowl. Refrigerate overnight to drain.

FRUIT COMPÔTES

Fresh fruit compôtes make great spreads for morning toast and afternoon scones. They're easy to make: the basic recipe can be adapted to any seasonal fruit that takes your fancy. The amount of sugar needed depends on the sweetness or tartness of the particular batch of fruit. You can always use a moderate amount of sugar, and then adjust the sweetness with NutraSweet after the compôte has cooled. Each recipe makes 1¼–1½ pints/700–900 ml of compôte.

Cherry

2 pints/1.1 litres stemmed, pitted,
    halved cherries (stem and pit
    them over a jug so that you catch
    all the juices)
2 tablespoons caster sugar
Pinch salt

1 tablespoon cornflour
2 tablespoons fresh orange juice
Slivered zest of ½ small lemon
Slivered zest of ½ small orange
½ teaspoon natural vanilla essence

Combine all the ingredients in a non-reactive saucepan. Cook slowly on top of the stove until thick and juicy. The fruit should be tender, but retain its shape. Cool.

Peach

2 pints/1.1 litres chunked peaches,
unpeeled (cut into chunks over a
    jug so that you catch all the juices)
2 tablespoons caster sugar
Pinch salt

1 tablespoon cornflour
2 tablespoons fresh orange juice
Slivered zest of ½ small lemon
Slivered zest of ½ small orange
½ teaspoon natural vanilla essence

Combine all the ingredients in a non-reactive saucepan. Cook slowly on the top of the stove until thick and juicy. The fruit should be tender, but retain its shape. Cool.

Plum–Peach

2 pints/1.1 litres pitted,
    chunked, unpeeled plums
    (about 1 lb 12 oz/ 800 g)
1 pint/570 ml pitted, chunked,
    unpeeled peaches (pit and chunk
    the fruits over a bowl so that you
    catch all the juices)
1 tablespoon cornflour
Pinch salt

4–5 tablespoons light brown sugar
Slivered zest of ½ lemon and
    ½ orange
1 teaspoon natural vanilla essence
3 tablespoons fresh orange juice

Combine all the ingredients in a non-reactive saucepan. Cook slowly on the top of the stove until thick and juicy. The fruit should be tender, but retain its shape. Cool.

Apricot–Peach

1½ pints/900 ml unpeeled apricots,
    pitted and quartered
½ pint/300 ml unpeeled peaches,
    pitted and quartered (pit and
    chunk the fruits over a jug so that
    you catch all the juices)
1 tablespoon cornflour

Pinch salt
3–5 tablespoons light brown sugar
Slivered zest of ½ orange and
    ½ lemon
1 teaspoon natural vanilla essence
1 tablespoon Amaretto liqueur

Combine all the ingredients in a non-reactive saucepan. Cook slowly on the top of the stove until thick and juicy. The fruit should be tender, but retain its shape. Cool.

Blueberry

1½ pints/900 ml blueberries,
    rinsed and dried
3–4 tablespoons caster sugar
Pinch salt

1 tablespoon cornflour
½ tablespoon lemon juice
Pinch each cinnamon and nutmeg

Combine all the ingredients in a non-reactive saucepan. Cook slowly on the top of the stove until thick and juicy. The fruit should be tender, but retain its shape. Cool.

Gooseberry

1½ pints/900 ml gooseberries,
    rinsed and dried
6 tablespoons caster sugar
Pinch salt

1 tablespoon cornflour
1 tablespoon orange juice
Pinch each cinnamon and nutmeg
NutraSweet as needed

Combine all the ingredients in a non-reactive saucepan. Cook slowly on the top of the stove until thick and juicy. The fruit should be tender, but retain its shape. Cool. Taste and stir in NutraSweet if the compôte is very tart.

Have a Bagel with Your Morning Coffee

A bagel is a dense, round roll with a hole in the middle. A true bagel is chewy – almost tough – in fact it has been described as a doughnut with rigor mortis. A split bagel (see box, page 77) spread with quark, chestnut cream, fruit compôte, or honeyed cream will light up your morning. My family and I journey to the Bagel Bakery on Brick Lane in London's East End every few months to buy dozens of bagels to take home for the freezer. A frozen bagel, wrapped in foil and placed in a 400°F, 200°C, Gas Mark 6 oven, takes 15–20 minutes to thaw. It emerges piping hot and tastes freshly baked. Some of the larger supermarkets have taken to stocking bagels (six to a plastic bag), and local bakeries here and there throughout the country are starting to bake them too.

I love the story of how the bagel originated. (It may be apocryphal, but it sure is romantic.)

In 1683 Prince Sobiesky of Poland rescued Vienna from Turkish invaders. When the Turks fled, they left everything behind except the clothes they wore and the horses on which they scarpered. Among the things left behind were cattle and sheep and their feed, tents, camels and hundreds of sacks full of small hard greenish oval beans. The Viennese assumed these odd beans to be camel feed, and a bonfire was begun to dispose of them. An alert Polish adventurer-spy knew better and snatched the wealth of coffee beans from the flames. As reward for a previous act of heroism, the Pole was given the coffee and a charter to open what would become Vienna's first coffee house. At first, the Viennese loathed the Turkish brew: it was too strong, too black, and much too muddy. But the resourceful Pole strained the coffee to eliminate the sediment, sweetened the strong liquid with honey and lightened it with milk. The Viennese loved it, as people all over the world love it today.

But, according to legend, something even more important than Viennese coffee was born in that long-ago coffee house. In honour of Prince Sobiesky, the Pole had special rolls baked in the shape of the Prince's stirrup. The rolls were given the German name, *Beugel* (stirrup). These – so I've been told – were the world's first bagels.

First, Split Your Bagel

Never use a knife to split a bagel. Proper bagel behaviour demands a fork. With the tines of a fork, perforate the bagel all around its outer perimeter. Then separate the bagel into two halves along the dotted line. Halved in this manner, the texture of the inner surface of each bagel half will be rough and absolutely delicious, whether spread with plain quark, one of the honeyed creams, or fruit compôte. Cut with a knife, the surface will be perfectly smooth and the bagel will be insipid. (It may even be flecked with blood if your knife-wielding technique is less than impeccable.)

Tea Time

Afternoon tea: I put it right up there with shepherd's pie, summer pudding, heated towel racks, London taxi drivers and the English National Opera. Yes, they told me England was a civilized place to live – they told me and they were *right*. Earl Grey Tea, cucumber sandwiches, sweet biscuits, clotted cream . . . er – wait a sec. Civilization is one thing, galloping schmaltz is another. I don't mean to dabble in things that are none of my business – I am a foreigner after all. Fiddling around with one's host country's gastronomic traditions can be downright insulting. But I mean to be neither arrogant nor insulting, I simply want to be able to enjoy the culinary ritual of afternoon tea without suffering its fattening consequences. What follows are several suggestions for very low-fat (but high pleasure) tea-time treats. Enjoy them in good health.

APPLE–SULTANA BUNS

Makes 24

Of course these would be terrific for breakfast as well as tea. They are very moist and fruity and keep exceptionally well if stored in an airtight tin. Split them and spread with one of the honeyed creams (page 81), a fruit compôte (page 74) or plain fromage frais.

2 Granny Smith apples, peeled, cored and very coarsely grated	1 teaspoon cinnamon
6 fl oz/175 ml fresh orange juice	Pinch nutmeg
1 teaspoon lemon juice	½ oz/10 g wheat bran
7 oz/200 g self-raising whole wheat cake flour	8 fl oz/225 ml buttermilk
3 oz/75 g sugar	1 tablespoon natural vanilla essence
	4–5 tablespoons sultanas

1   Preheat the oven to 375°F, 190°C, Gas Mark 5.
2   Combine the apples, orange juice and lemon juice.
3   Sift together the flour, sugar, cinnamon and nutmeg. Stir in the bran.
4   Stir in the buttermilk and vanilla. Do not beat and do not overmix or the muffins will be tough. The batter should be a bit lumpy.
5   *Very gently* fold in the apples and their juice, and the sultanas.
6   Spoon the batter into two light-coloured, non-stick bun tins. Bake for 25–30 minutes, until golden and cooked through but still moist. Cool the bun tins on racks for 5–10 minutes, before gently loosening each bun with a palette knife, and removing from the tin.

'Oh for a good cup of tea! A truly British cry that I echo so often in my travels around four o'clock in the afternoon. Tea is my panacea, my consolation, if you will, my 'fix' . . . If there is one meal that I could repeat during the day – without getting fat, of course – it would be tea . . . One can sit down comfortably without feeling that one's wasting time, take stock and gear oneself up for the rest of the day.'
Diana Kennedy, *Nothing Fancy*

SCONES

Makes approximately 9

Yes, I know – these are a bit eccentric for scones. But they are tender, lovely and sweet. Maize meal is sprinkled on the baking sheet to keep them from sticking; the meal has the advantage of giving the scones a delightfully slightly crunchy bottom. You can use either maize meal or polenta (which is simply a form of maize meal). (See Mail Order Guide, page 133, for both.)

1 lb/450 g self-raising sponge flour   *Brown sugar (optional)*
Pinch salt   *Pinch cinnamon (optional)*
½–1 pint/300–570 ml buttermilk   *Maize meal*
2 tablespoons runny honey

1   Put the flour into a large bowl. Sprinkle the salt over it. Make a well in the middle of the flour.

2   Pour ½ pint/300 ml buttermilk into the well. With a wooden spoon, stir the flour into the buttermilk. Add the honey and more buttermilk as needed to form a rather rough, slightly sticky dough. Switch from the spoon to both hands, and knead for a few turns. The dough should remain slightly sticky and rough. Don't overwork the dough or the scones will be tough. Sprinkle some flour on a sheet of waxed or greaseproof paper.

3   Pull lumps of dough and form into rough balls about the size of tennis balls. If they are hard to handle because they are so sticky, dip lightly into the flour, but be careful to treat them gently so they will not be tough. Again, don't overwork them; they should be lumpy. Sprinkle a non-stick baking pan with maize meal. Evenly space the balls on the pan. If you wish, sprinkle each ball with a pinch of brown sugar and cinnamon. Bake in a 400°F, 200°C, Gas Mark 6 oven for 30–35 minutes. When they are done, they sound hollow when tapped on the bottom.

     Eat hot, warm, or at room temperature. To serve, split in half and heap each half with fruit compôte or jam – top with fromage frais, or with any of the honeyed creams (page 81). Or serve spread with fromage frais and heaped with fresh berries.

THUMBPRINT COOKIES

Makes 20 cookies

Talk about ambiguity. An American food writer, living and working in England, traverses a minefield of possible confusions during every working moment. What an English person calls a scone, an American calls a biscuit. Well, you do have biscuits too, but where I come from, they're called cookies. So the recipe that follows is for crunchy little thumbprint *biscuits*, designed so that their thumbprint depressions can be filled with one of the Slim Cuisine creams – Chestnut Cream, Honeyed Vanilla Cream, Banana

Cream . . . Drat! They are *not* biscuits. They are *cookies*, do you hear – *cookies*! Eat these cookies for tea with your biscuits – I mean your scones. Was it George Bernard Shaw who said that England and America are two countries divided by a common language? How right he was! Anyway, however you refer to these delightful little cream-filled morsels, you are sure to enjoy them.

3 oz/75 g amaretti biscuits, crushed	*2 oz/50 g Grape-Nuts cereal, crushed* *2 egg whites*

1   Preheat the oven to 375°F, 190°C, Gas Mark 5.
2   Combine all the ingredients thoroughly in a bowl.
3   Choose a non-stick baking sheet. Take 1 teaspoon of the mixture and roll into a ball. Flatten each ball on to the non-stick baking sheet. Using your thumb, make a depression with a raised edge in each cookie. Bake for 20–30 minutes (depends on the humidity) until dry and crispy. Cool on a rack.
    The cookies may be served as they are, or the thumbprint depression may be filled with a piped (use a piping bag) or spooned mixture: Chocolate Pudding, Banana Mousse, one of the cheesecake fillings, Chestnut Cream, etc.

MERINGUE COOKIES

Makes 100

If you bake these on a humid or rainy day, they will never quite dry out – there will be that slight sticky-gooiness in the centre. Of course, many people prefer them that way.

3 egg whites at room temperature *Pinch each of cream of tartar and salt*	*5 oz/150 g sugar* *1 teaspoon natural vanilla essence*

1   Preheat the oven to 225°F, 120°C, Gas Mark 1.
2   Beat the egg whites with the cream of tartar and salt until foamy. Increase speed. Beat, adding sugar, 1–2 tablespoons at a time, until the whites are shiny and stiff and hold firm peaks. Fold in the vanilla.
3   Line two baking sheets with silicone paper. Drop the batter on the sheets by the ½ teaspoonful, 1 inch/2.5 cm apart. Bake for 45 minutes.

4   Turn the oven off. Leave the meringues in the oven for at least 3 hours. (They can stay in overnight.) Do not open the door until the time is up. Store in an airtight tin.

⊕ HONEYED VANILLA CREAM

Yields 18 fl oz/475 ml

Honey and the pulp of a vanilla bean give fragrant character to fromage frais. Use clouds of the aromatic cream on fruit and berries, on slices of Angel Cake and Stir Crazy Torte (pages 60 and 63), or with Maren's Fruit Dumplings (page 48). Both of these creams may be drained overnight in a muslin-lined sieve over a bowl. They then can be spread on bread, or piped through a piping bag to decorate cakes and tortes.

---

1 vanilla pod
1 lb 2 oz/500 g very low-fat
    fromage frais
2 tablespoons runny honey

---

1   With a small, sharp knife, split the vanilla pod lengthwise. With the tip of the knife, scrape out the soft inside of both halves. Scrape the material into the fromage frais. (Save the scraped pod to store in a jar of granulated NutraSweet or a canister of caster sugar. It will impart its fragrance to the sweetener.)

2   Stir the honey into the fromage frais. Stir so that the black vanilla bean specks are evenly distributed through the fromage frais. Store in the refrigerator.

♡ Substitute NutraSweet for the honey.

⊕ *Variation*: Honeyed Almond Cream

Yields 18 fl oz/475 ml

---

1 teaspoon natural vanilla essence	*1 lb 2 oz/500 g very low-fat*
½ teaspoon natural almond essence	*fromage frais*
	2 tablespoons runny honey

Combine all the ingredients in a bowl. Stir until they are all thoroughly blended. Store in refrigerator.

A Gift from the Bees

Honey is a form of sugar and therefore a basically 'empty Calorie' (no nutrients to speak of) food, but a little bit goes a long way, as far as lovely taste and sweetening power are concerned. Honey is an ancient food; since the Stone Age, humankind has depended on it to sweeten food, and – often – to improve life as well. A Roman senator advised Julius Caesar: 'Eat honey and lengthen your life.' (Alas, ambition and intrigue shortened Caesar's life, not a dearth of honey.) Fifteen centuries later, about the time of the Renaissance, European mothers believed that copious amounts of honey taken during pregnancy helped shape a docile, sweet-natured child. Even today, honey is used symbolically and as an energy source. During New Year's celebrations, Jewish families dip slices of apple and chunks of bread into honey to ensure a sweet year. And I have heard that dancers at the Bolshoi consume globs of the stuff just before the curtain rises – it's quick energy they're after.

We all know that honey is produced by bees, but how exactly is it made, anyway? I must say, the whole process is a bit off-putting, if fascinating. A bee collects nectar from flowers and transports it – in the bee's honey sac – to the hive. As the bee rushes from flower to hive, his digestive fluids begin to break down the nectar's sugars. At the hive, the bee regurgitates the nectar into the mouths of young bees. (I *told* you it was off-putting!) The young bees breathe on the nectar to concentrate it, and at the same time their secretions cause further changes in its chemical structures. Finally, the nectar is spat into the storage cells of the hive, where it concentrates even further, and – finally – becomes thick, sweet *honey*. There are as many varieties as there are kinds of flower nectars for bees to feast upon. Wild thyme honey, orange blossom, sage, rosemary, apple blossom – the names themselves are intoxicating.

'And is there honey still for tea?'
Rupert Brooke, *The Old Vicarage, Grantchester*

Cold Comfort

'Marshmallow mint, peach–strawberry ripple, lemon–
cherry whirl, chocolate fudge, chocolate chip, chocolate
walnut, chocolate rum, and classic vanilla, of course – the
purest, the most ethereal of tastes . . . Glynnis springs to
her feet, hurries out into the kitchen, and returns, gaily,
with an armful of quart containers of ice cream, seven
dramatically different flavours: tosses down spoons, tells
her friends to taste, to sample, to pass the containers
around – "We needn't bother with bowls" . . .
So, like children, they pass the containers around:
protesting, some of them, that they cannot eat another
mouthful of anything, yet spooning up the ice cream
nonetheless; like children.'

Joyce Carol Oates, *American Appetites*

I Scream, You Scream,
We All Scream for Ice Cream

Ice cream is often considered a treat for children only, but historically speaking, nothing is further from the truth. Until relatively recently, ice cream was considered a sophisticated adult food. In Europe, it began in the thirteenth century, when Marco Polo came home from the Chinese Court bearing, among other things, a recipe for water ices. The Italian aristocracy loved the icy confection, but it wasn't until the fourteenth century that someone thought to add milk and eggs to the basic recipe. The addition resulted – as you can imagine – in a seductive creaminess. In 1533 the youth who was to become France's King Henry II married the young Italian Catherine De Medici. Catherine brought a culinary dowry to France that included fine chefs, porcelain, cookware, exotic ingredients, and elegant recipes. Among her Italian ideas and ingredients were quenelles, sweetbreads, veal, artichoke hearts – and ice cream. For each day of the wedding celebration, the chefs prepared a new flavour. French royalty revelled in the ice cream, but it didn't reach the plain folk until 1660, when a Sicilian named Francesco Procopio opened the Café Procope in Paris. Suddenly ice cream was the talk of Paris.

By the eighteenth century ice cream reached England, and soon America, establishing itself in the New World, picked up the thread. George Washington, America's first president, heard about ice cream from Alexander Hamilton's wife. Washington promptly purchased two ice cream pots: pewter vessels in which the ingredients were combined, beaten by hand, and agitated in a surrounding bath of ice and salt, until the proper creamy, frozen consistency was achieved. But it took a woman to really get things going. In 1846, an American named Nancy Johnson invented the hand-cranked ice cream freezer. The awkward pewter pots became obsolete, and ice cream, ceremoniously hand-cranked at home, became an American delicacy. In 1851 in Baltimore, the first commercial ice cream business was established; in 1874 in Philadelphia, the ice cream soda was born; and in 1904, at the St Louis World's Fair, a quick-thinking Syrian–American waffle vendor invented the ice cream cone. Ice cream, which had begun as ultra-sophisticated gastronomic exotica in the royal courts of Europe, now belonged to everyone, especially to the children.

'The only emperor is the emperor of ice cream.'
Wallace Steven, *The Emperor of Ice Cream*

Home-made Ice Cream

The old fashioned hand-cranked ice cream machine, with its reservoir for salt and ice, has become as obsolete as the pewter ice cream pots of the eighteenth century. You can now buy an expensive and elegant machine that contains its own freezing unit. Pour in your ice cream mix, push the button, and – in about 30 minutes – your ice cream is ready. I'm glad to say that there is an equally elegant machine available that is not expensive at all. It does not contain its own freezing unit, but it is designed to go directly into your home freezer. Pour in the ice cream mix and – as with the pricey machine – home-made ice cream in 30 minutes. What a change from messing about with ice and rock salt and hand-cranks. Does it pay to buy your own machine? Yes indeed, if you like ice cream, and if you care about your health and your weight. With your own machine, you can have ice cream whenever you like, as often as you like, and you can control exactly what goes into it.

Commercial ice creams contain plenty of sugar and much too much fat for a fat-prone person to eat with prudence. Inexpensive ice creams tend to contain a distressing amount of fillers and generally unattractive ingredients; quality ice creams contain enough butterfat to choke a brontosaurus. My collection of ice creams are made with skimmed milk. The addition of skimmed milk powder to the skimmed milk adds an amazing richness to the ice cream. Don't assume that these ice creams (technically, they are not ice 'creams' at all – they contain no cream or full fat milk) will taste thin and insipid. Nothing is further from the truth. They have a pure, vivid creaminess that I think will delight you. They are at their creamiest right after they are made, or stored in the freezer for an hour or so. If they stay frozen overnight, they turn fairly hard. In that case, let them stand on the kitchen counter for 15 minutes or so before scooping.

❄ VANILLA ICE CREAM

The vanilla ice cream of my New York childhood – the kind scooped and pressed into crunchy sugar cones at the corner mom and pop 'candy store' or plopped into chilled silvery dishes at Schraffts – had a clean fresh purity unmatched by the vanilla ice creams of today. Today's quality vanilla ice creams are marred by their too-high butterfat level which – to my mind – destroys the purity of taste and leaves a cloying, underlying fattiness on the palate. Cheap vanilla ice creams are destroyed by synthetic vanilla flavouring (very harsh and unpleasant) and the stabilizers and fillers used in the product (read the labels next time you pass the supermarket freezer case). My vanilla ice cream is a return to innocence: virtually no butterfat, no stabilizers, pure vanilla. Some people, once they taste the purity of *real* vanilla ice cream, never want to venture further. Coffee ice cream, chocolate, strawberry, don't interest them one iota: they know vanilla is best, and they never budge from that belief. Try this and see what you think.

16 fl oz/425 ml skimmed milk *6–8 tablespoons skimmed milk* *powder* *3 oz/75 g sugar*	*1 teaspoon natural vanilla essence,* *or the scrapings from 1 vanilla* *pod (see page 16)*

1   Combine all the ingredients in a jug and mix until the sugar is dissolved.
2   Pour into the canister of an ice cream machine and proceed according to the manufacturer's directions.

❋ CHOCOLATE ICE CREAM

Makes 1¼ pints/700 ml

I have to admit it: I love vanilla ice cream, but I hear that chocolate calling to me. Innocence is great, but please give me some chocolate to go with it.

16 fl oz/425 ml skimmed milk *4 tablespoons low fat, unsweetened* *cocoa powder (see Mail Order* *Guide, page 133)*	*3 oz/75 g caster sugar* *1 teaspoon natural vanilla essence* *8 tablespoons dried skimmed milk* *powder*

1   Gently heat the milk to just before boiling point. Dissolve the cocoa in the milk. Whisk well.
2   Pour through a sieve into a bowl. Add the remaining ingredients and whisk well.
3   Pour into the ice cream maker. Freeze according to the manufacturer's directions.

❄ COFFEE ICE CREAM

Use best-quality filter or plunger coffee only. If you are anti-caffeine, use filter or plunger water-process decaffeinated coffee. Try serving a coffee-cup sundae: a pool of Hot Chocolate Sauce (page 96), several scoops of Coffee Ice Cream, and a sprinkled topping of mixed Grape-Nuts cereal and crumbled amaretti biscuits. Serve in your prettiest coffee cups.

8 fl oz/225 ml coffee	*3 oz/75 g sugar*
8 fl oz/225 ml skimmed milk	*½ teaspoon natural vanilla essence*
8 tablespoons skimmed milk powder	

1   Combine all the ingredients in a jug and mix until the sugar is dissolved.
2   Pour into the canister of an ice cream machine and proceed according to the manufacturer's directions.

❄ AMARETTI ICE CREAM

Makes 1 pint/570 ml

Crunchy amaretti biscuits, crumbled into basic vanilla, make a delicious almond-haunted ice cream. As with all Slim Cuisine ice creams, the texture is very creamy but without the slightest bit of cloying fattiness.

16 fl oz/425 ml skimmed milk	*1 teaspoon natural vanilla essence*
8 tablespoons skimmed milk powder	*4 amaretti biscuits*
1 tablespoon sugar	

1   Combine all the ingredients in a jug except for 2 amaretti, and mix until the sugar is dissolved.
2   Pour into the canister of an ice cream machine and proceed according to the manufacturer's directions.
3   Sprinkle in another amaretti just before the ice cream is ready, and fold the last amaretti into the ice cream at the end.

❄ GRAPE-NUT ICE CREAM

Makes 1¼ pints/700 ml

There is a traditional dessert of New England called Grape-Nut Pudding. I lived in Cambridge, Massachusetts for several years and learned about this homely dish along with many other interesting things: the baked bean (I mean the *real* thing – not the stuff that comes in tins), the steamed brown bread, the lobster pie and the baked scrod. But I digress. The first time I had Grape-Nut Pudding I noticed these little nuggets in it. What on earth could they be? Grape-Nuts of course; something that I, sophisticated New York native that I was, had never heard of. I grew to love the toasted wheat and barley cereal, and learned to do what many New Englanders do: use them in all sorts of clever culinary ways, even – occasionally – for breakfast. Here, they contribute a most pleasing gentle crunchiness to brown sugar–cinnamon ice cream.

16 fl oz/425 ml skimmed milk	2 tablespoons Grape-Nuts cereal
8 tablespoons skimmed milk powder	1 teaspoon ground cinnamon
2 oz/50 g sugar	½ tablespoon brown sugar
1 teaspoon natural vanilla essence	

1   Combine all the ingredients in a jug and mix until the sugar is dissolved.
2   Pour into the canister of an ice cream machine and proceed according to the manufacturer's directions.

❄ BANANA ICE CREAM

Makes 2 pints/1.1 litres

For banana fans, this ice cream is satisfyingly banana-y. For a total banana experience, serve scoops of it on servings of piping hot Grilled Bananas and Rum (page 52), or on wedges of Stir Crazy Banana–Fudge Torte (page 64).

16 fl oz/425 ml skimmed milk	½ teaspoon cinnamon
8 tablespoons skimmed milk powder	4 grilled bananas (see page 53)
1 oz/25 g sugar	1 tablespoon orange concentrate
1 teaspoon natural vanilla essence	

1   Combine all the ingredients in the container of a food processor. Process until perfectly smooth.
2. Pour into the canister of an ice cream machine and proceed according to the manufacturer's directions.

❄ BRENDA'S STRAWBERRY FROZEN YOGHURT

Makes ¾ pint/400 ml

Frozen yoghurt is the newest creamy cold confection to hit the popular market. It has become a craze in North America, and – I suspect – will catch on in a big way in the UK as well. Very low-fat frozen fruit yoghurts, and soft frozen yoghurts, are already available from supermarkets, delicatessens and up-market sand-wich shops here and there. If you have an ice cream machine you can easily make your own. One of my helpers, Brenda Huebler, developed this one. Her idea of combining very low-fat yoghurt with fromage frais is excellent; the finished product has a very pleasant slight yoghurt tanginess but it is in no way over-powering.

6 oz/175 ml strawberries	*7 fl oz/200 ml natural skimmed*
2 oz/50 g caster sugar	*milk yoghurt*
Juice of ½ lemon	*1½ fl oz/38 ml fromage frais*

1   Wash the fruit and mash it with the sugar.
2   Mix the lemon juice with the yoghurt.
3   Combine all the ingredients together with the fromage frais. Freeze in an ice cream machine according to the manufac-turer's directions.

> *'Abraham drank it. Some authorities attribute Sarah's reproductive cycle to it. Solomon's wisdom came from the consumption of it. Yoghurt, of course!'*
> Joan Nathan, *The Jewish Holiday Kitchen*

❄ BERRY–BANANA FROZEN YOGHURT

Makes 1¾ pints/1 litre

This recipe, and the two that follow, combine fruit (each recipe includes a ripe banana for textural richness) with skimmed milk yoghurt and fromage frais. The exact amount of sugar to use depends on the sweetness of the fruit, so always taste the mixture, and sweeten accordingly.

1½ pints/900 ml mixed berries (raspberries, blackberries, blueberries) 1 very ripe banana Approximately 3 oz/75 g light brown sugar	¼ pint/150 ml frozen orange juice concentrate 1 teaspoon natural vanilla essence 6 fl oz/150 ml skimmed milk yoghurt 6 fl oz/150 ml fromage frais

1   Purée the berries in the food processor, then sieve to remove the seeds.
2   Purée the banana in the processor. Add the puréed and sieved berries, the sugar, orange juice concentrate, and vanilla. Pulse on and off to blend. Add the yoghurt and fromage frais. Pulse again a few times to blend.
3   Freeze in the ice cream machine according to the manufacturer's directions. (You may – for some machines – have to do it in two batches.) Eat at once, or store in the freezer. After a sojourn in the freezer, the confection will be fairly hard. Let it stand on the kitchen counter for 15–20 minutes before scooping.

❄ PEACH–BANANA FROZEN YOGHURT

Makes 2½ pints/1.3 litres

1¾ pints/1 litre (approximately 2 lb/900 g) ripe peaches, peeled, stoned and cubed 1 very ripe banana, peeled and sliced Approximately 2 oz/50 g brown sugar	¼ pint/150 ml frozen orange juice concentrate 1 teaspoon natural vanilla essence 6 fl oz/150 ml low-fat yoghurt 6 fl oz/150 ml very low-fat fromage frais

1   Purée the fruit in the food processor.
2   Add the sugar, orange juice concentrate, and vanilla essence. Pulse on and off to blend. Add the yoghurt and fromage frais. Pulse again a few times to blend.
3   Freeze in the ice cream machine according to the manufacturer's directions. (You may – for some machines – have to do it in two batches.) Eat at once or store in the freezer. After a sojourn in the freezer, the confection will be quite hard. Let it stand on the kitchen counter for 30–40 minutes before scooping.

❄ PEAR–BANANA FROZEN YOGHURT

Makes 2 pints/1.1 litre

1½ pints/900 ml ripe pears, peeled, cored and cubed	¼ pint/150 ml frozen orange juice concentrate
1 very ripe banana, peeled and sliced	1 teaspoon natural vanilla essence
Approximately 3 oz/75 g brown sugar	6 fl oz/150 ml very low-fat yoghurt
	6 fl oz/150 ml very low-fat fromage frais

1   Purée the fruit in the food processor.
2   Add the sugar, orange concentrate, and vanilla. Pulse on and off to blend. Add the yoghurt and fromage frais. Pulse again a few times to blend.
3   Freeze in the ice cream machine according to the manufacturer's directions. (You may – for some machines – have to do it in two batches.) Eat at once or store in the freezer. After a sojourn in the freezer, the confection will be quite hard. Let it stand on the kitchen counter for 30–40 minutes before scooping.

Sodas and Sundaes

In an old-fashioned American ice cream parlour or soda fountain, ice cream sodas are made in tall, frosty glasses. First, flavoured syrup (coffee, chocolate, or vanilla) and milk are stirred together. Then soda water is squirted in forcefully from a siphon bottle while the soda jerk (no – I'm not making this up; he really is called a soda jerk) stirs like mad with a long-handled silver spoon. When the sweet foamy head all but overflows the tall glass, the soda jerk picks up his capacious scoop, and scoops up a huge serving of ice cream from an array of dozens of choices of flavours. The oversized ball of ice cream is then plopped on to the rim of the glass, half in, half out of the liquid. A generous dollop of whipped cream crowns the whole concoction. The ice cream soda is properly consumed in the following manner (this method was personally researched by *me*, time after time, starting about forty-five years ago):

1   Choose a paper-covered straw from the silvery straw dispenser on the counter. Carefully tear off the top of the paper covering, move the paper cover down the slightest bit, take aim at the nearest adult, and *blow*.
2   Immediately insert the straw into the soda and start sipping.

If the paper cover reached its target, look innocent and sip harder. If it does *not* reach its target and just – as often happens – falls to the counter limply, save it for later to pleat into intricate accordion shapes which will be invaluable for dabbling into the soda puddles on the counter when your soda is all finished.

3   Through the straw, take several deep sips of the delicious sparkly, creamy liquid in the glass. Lean right down and take a large mouthful of the whipped cream. Make sure everyone notices your amusing whipped cream moustache and whipped-cream-daubed nose.

4   With your spoon, dig into the ball of ice cream, and consume – with much licking and grinning – a large spoonful. The ice cream, of course, will topple from the rim of the glass into the soda with a most satisfying splash. That is exactly as it should be. Continue demolishing the ice cream soda by alternating straw and spoon, with occasional brief pauses to swipe at your mouth with a handful of white paper napkins pulled from the dispenser on the counter.

5   When the soda is *almost* gone, push the straw right into the luscious puddle of soda, syrup and melted ice cream in the bottom of the glass. Suck up every lovely bit through the straw. The clattering, sucking noise is *brilliant*! If this noise does not occur, you haven't done the job properly.

The hard part was deciding which to have in the first place – a soda or a sundae. The sundae was invented in the early twentieth century because of American 'blue laws', the laws that determined what was allowed and what was not on Sunday. For some reason, the blue laws of the time decreed soda water inappropriate to the Sabbath. Since a favourite Sunday occupation of families in middle America was – after church – to wander over to the soda fountain for a refreshing ice cream soda, the proprietors of such establishments were in a quandary. How to satisfy their customers' cravings, without exposing them to profane soda water on the Lord's day? With true American ingenuity they invented a new delicacy: the ice cream soda *without* soda. First ice cream was generously scooped into a silvery dish. Then a heavenly rich sauce was ladled over – perhaps hot fudge, or chunky pineapple, or crushed strawberry, or marshmallow cream . . . Finally dollops of whipped cream were billowed on top, and a cherry crowned the whole thing. The glorious concoction was named for the day – Sunday – but the 'y' was changed to an 'e' so that the name of the Sabbath was not taken in vain. Thus was an enduring and beloved classic born.

❄ CHOCOLATE SORBET

Makes 1 pint/570 ml

This is not an ice cream; it contains no dairy products at all, just sugar, water and low-fat cocoa powder. Chocoholics take note: this is a *deep, meaningful* chocolate experience. It will strike you speechless. To call it *intensely chocolatey* does not begin to describe its impact.

8 oz/225 g granulated sugar (see note)	2 oz/50 g unsweetened low-fat cocoa (see Mail Order Guide, page 133)
18 fl oz/475 ml water	½ teaspoon natural vanilla essence

1   Combine the sugar and water in a saucepan and heat gently until the sugar has dissolved. Raise the heat and boil for 1 minute. Remove from the heat and allow to cool a bit.
2   Stir a little of the sugar–water syrup into the cocoa in a bowl, to make a smooth paste, then gradually stir in the remaining syrup.
3   Add the vanilla. Strain the mixture through a fine sieve.
4   Freeze in an ice cream maker, following the manufacturer's instructions.

Note: For a sorbet that is lower in sugar Calories, use 6 oz/180 g granulated sugar and 2 tablespoons NutraSweet. Follow the recipe above, but add the NutraSweet after the syrup has cooled. This version freezes *harder* than the full-sugar one, and will have to stand at room temperature for a few minutes to soften before serving.

♡ ⊕ SLIM CUISINE FOOD PROCESSOR ICE CREAMS

I've written about this basic technique often (in every Slim Cuisine book in fact); I've demonstrated it on television; I've described it on the radio; and I've included it in food classes all around the country. I can hardly, therefore, pretend it's new: in fact it's becoming something of a cliché. But I can't help myself: I *must* include it here. This technique results in an instant, no-fuss, no-fat, no-sugar, high-fibre and nutrient-dense ice cream. Oh – and by the way – it's absolutely delicious. To prepare this ice cream you will need frozen berries or frozen cubes of fruit. Prepare them this way: place berries or fruit cubes – in one layer – on non-stick baking trays, in the freezer. When solidly frozen, place the berries or fruit cubes in plastic bags and store in the freezer until needed. Always keep plenty of frozen fruit of all varieties in the freezer. When you pull out a bag, if the cubes have frozen together into one big clump, knock the clump sharply on the kitchen counter a few times to separate.

You will also need buttermilk (see page 17), granulated Nutra-Sweet and natural vanilla essence (or vanilla NutraSweet, see page 16).

To prepare the ice cream, dump some *still frozen* berries or fruit cubes in the container of a food processor. How much depends on how much ice cream you want to make. Sprinkle in just a small bit of NutraSweet, unless the fruit is very sweet (mango, pineapple, and very ripe banana, for instance, often need no added sweetener at all). Add a dash of natural vanilla essence. Pour in a bit of buttermilk (2–3 fl oz/50–75 ml per approximately 12 oz/350 g of fruit). Turn on the machine. Don't be alarmed: the machine will rattle and clatter and vibrate all over the counter. These machines were designed to crush ice if necessary, so you will do no damage – let it clatter for a minute or two. Turn off the machine, scrape down the sides, then process again, pouring in another 2–3 fl oz/ 50–75 ml of buttermilk. Process for another minute or two, stop and scrape down the sides again, and taste for sweetness. Add more NutraSweet if necessary, then process until the mixture forms a smooth, beautifully creamy ice cream. You may have to stop and scrape it down another time or two – it depends on your machine. If you wish, at this point you may add some *fresh* fruit, cut into chunks, to the mixture. Pulse the machine on and off 2–3 times to chop the fruit, and to incorporate it into the ice cream, but don't process it enough to pulverize it. The resulting fruity bits within the smooth cream are quite enchanting – especially with peach or strawberry ice cream.

As soon as this ice cream is processed, it is ready to be eaten. It can wait in the freezer for an hour if necessary – any longer and it gets very hard. Even if you then let it stand on the counter for a while, it never regains its original glorious creaminess. So when you feel the urge, pull out the machine, grab a bag of fruit pieces from the freezer, and presto: ice cream in less than 5 minutes.

I've been making this ice cream for years and I never get tired of it; in fact, it never ceases to amaze me. You start with a mass of solidly frozen fruit and a dribble of buttermilk – in minutes it has changed to a perfectly gorgeous mound of creamy, vividly fruity ice cream.

⊕ ⊠ HOT CHOCOLATE SAUCE

Makes approximately ¾ pint/400 ml

Rich, thick and velvety, this sauce is lovely poured over chocolate or coffee ice cream for the classic 'cold as winter, hot as summer' effect of a hot fudge sundae. The sauce is good cold as well.

2 tablespoons low-fat, unsweetened cocoa powder (see Mail Order Guide, page 133)	2–3 tablespoons sugar
	12 fl oz/350 ml skimmed milk
	1 tablespoon skimmed milk powder
2 tablespoons cornflour	

1   Combine all the ingredients in a liquidizer container, and blend until perfectly smooth. Pour into a 3-pint/1.8-litre bowl or jug and cover tightly with microwave-safe cling film.
2   Microwave on full power until the mixture comes to a boil (about 4 minutes). Prick the cling film to release the steam, carefully remove the film, and stir the sauce with a wooden spoon.

⊕ BAKED BANANA, RUM, RAISIN SAUCE FOR ICE CREAM

Serves 1 (make as many packets as you need)

I'm very, very pleased indeed with my method for making hot banana, rum, raisin sauce. The ingredients are baked – in a hot oven – in folded, crimped parchment packets. What fun when each guest – waiting with his or her portion of home-made vanilla ice cream – is handed a hot, puffy, steaming, odorous package and a pair of scissors. Snip the end of the packet and slide the contents on to the ice cream. Eat fast with a big spoon. Bliss!

1 ripe banana	Pinch brown sugar
1 tablespoon each: dark rum, lemon juice, lime juice, orange juice	½ tablespoon raisins

1   Preheat the oven to 425°F, 220°C, Gas Mark 7.
2   Cut the bananas in half lengthwise, then cut crosswise into ½-inch/1.25-cm chunks. Put the bananas on the bottom half of a piece of folded parchment paper (see diagram).
3   Evenly sprinkle all the remaining ingredients over the bananas. Fold and crimp the parchment packet all around so that no steam can escape (see diagram).

Afternoon tea in the garden: scones with fruit compôte and
honeyed vanilla cream.

Winter comfort: clockwise from bottom left: apple-raisin flan;
winter pudding; fruit soufflé.

Delights of summer: clockwise from lower left: summer pudding; cherries in strawberry sauce; strawberry mousse; strawberry *coeur à la crème* with strawberry coulis.

You may have your cake, and stay slim too! White angel cake,
and black and white angel cake.

4   Put the packet on a baking sheet and bake for 10 minutes. The packet will become browned and puffy.
5   Serve each diner a hot, puffy packet, a pair of scissors and a portion of vanilla ice cream. Let them cut open the ends of their packets and then tip out the bananas and juices over the ice cream.

♡ Omit the sugar and raisins.

Fold down one corner.

Start a second fold so that it incorporates a bit of the first fold.

Continue folding and crimping all around until

the banana is well secured and no steam or juice can escape.

Make sure you leave space on top so that the paper does not touch the top surface of the banana.

♡ ⊕ ❄ FRUIT COULIS

This method works beautifully with fresh, or frozen and thawed, fruits and berries. Try mango, peaches, raspberries, blueberries, strawberries, tayberries, blackcurrants, blackberries . . . Strawberry Coulis is particularly glorious with Chocolate Sorbet (page 94).

Purée the fruit or berries in the processor or liquidizer. If the fruit or berries are particularly fibrous or contain pips, sieve the purée. Sweeten to taste with NutraSweet. If the taste needs sharpening, squeeze in just a bit of lemon juice. Refrigerate until needed.

⊕ Fruit Rickeys

Old-fashioned soda fountains sold fruit rickeys in addition to milkshakes and ice cream sodas, but most kids weren't interested – they preferred the over-the-top cream-laden excesses of the shakes and sodas to the tart refreshment of the rickeys. But for an adult (and for discerning children) a fruit rickey (sometimes called a fruit shrub) is a wonderful treat. To make one, pour some fruit coulis (see above) or some citrus juice (orange juice or sweetened lemon or lime juice) into the bottom of a tall, chilled glass. Pour in very cold sparkling water, stirring all the while. Press a generous scoop of fruit sorbet (see index) on to the rim of the glass. Provide a long straw, and a long-handled spoon. Now that we seem to be having long, hot English summers, this is the perfect tall, cold drink to enjoy on steamy days.

♡ Sweeten the citrus juice with NutraSweet. Use food processor sorbets (page 103).

♡ ⊠VANILLA MILKSHAKE

Makes approximately 3 pints/1.7 litres

I'm reprinting this here from *The Slim Cuisine Diet* because it's so *good*. In smaller quantities the vanilla shake can be used as a whipped-cream-type topping for ice cream sundaes, ice cream sodas and any desserts that would benefit from a creamy dollop or two. (If you are preparing it as whipped cream, rather than a shake, halve or quarter the recipe.)

---

1 pint/570 ml skimmed milk slush (see note)
6 tablespoons skimmed milk powder

2 tablespoons vanilla NutraSweet (see page 16)

---

1   Combine about ¾ of the milk slush and all the remaining ingredients in a food processor.
2   Process until thick, the consistency of whipped cream, and greatly (unbelievably!) increased in bulk (at *least* 2 minutes of processing). The longer you process the mixture, the stiffer and more like whipped cream it becomes. Add the rest of the slush gradually, as it processes. Pour into cold glasses and serve at once, with spoons, or use as whipped 'cream' for berries, bananas, etc.

♡ *Variations:*

Coffee: as vanilla recipe above, except use ¾ the amount of milk slush, and add ¼ pint/150 ml coffee slush (see note).

Note: **To make skimmed milk slush**, freeze 1-pint cartons of long-life (UHT) skimmed milk. When you want to make a milk shake, remove the carton from the freezer, and – with scissors – cut off the top, and cut the carton away from the frozen block of milk. Put the milk into a microwave receptacle, and microwave on high for 2–3 minutes, until slushy and partially melted. With a spoon or a dull knife chop and mush up the milk until the texture is consistently slushy.
   To make coffee slush, store strong filter coffee in the freezer. Defrost in the microwave until slushy.

Mocha Variation:

Make the vanilla milkshake (see recipe above). When the mixture has become very thick, add – while the mixture is processing – ½–1 teaspoon instant espresso granules. When it is thoroughly amalgamated, taste and process in a light sprinkling of low fat cocoa powder and a bit more sweetener if necessary. Serve at once.

Note: If you do not have a microwave, freeze the milk, in its carton, until it is partially frozen and slushy. Proceed with the recipe as written.

♡ ▨ CHOCOLATE MILKSHAKE

Makes 3 pints/1.7 litres

---

1 pint/570 ml skimmed milk slush
(see note, page 99)
6 tablespoons skimmed milk powder
3 tablespoons vanilla NutraSweet
(see note, page 16)

2–3 rounded tablespoons of low-fat
unsweetened cocoa powder (see
Mail Order Guide, page 133)

---

1   Combine ¾ of the milk slush and all the remaining ingredients in a food processor.
2   Process until thick, the consistency of whipped cream, and greatly (unbelievably!) increased in bulk (at *least* 2 minutes of processing). The longer you process the mixture the stiffer and more like whipped cream it becomes. Pour into cold glasses and serve at once, with spoons.

'... I had a tuna-fish sandwich and a chocolate milk shake, my standard tranquilizer ...'
        Shelley Winters, *Best of Times, Worst of Times*

100

The Song of the Soda Jerk

'What have I got? You want to know what I've got? I'll tell you what I've got. I've got ice creams that you could die for. This is the place where ice cream is serious business.

If you want to give your taste buds a run for their money, then by golly you've come to the right place. What we give you here is the ice cream of your dreams.

You want a soda? I got the grand-daddy of all soda right here: the Egg Cream. No egg, no cream, but that's what it's called. Go figure it out! If it's a taste of paradise you want, this is what you go for. You take a glass (and I mean a BIG glass) and you pour in some chocolate syrup. Don't worry about putting in too much, life is too short, right? Then some milk. Now the important part: your good solid seltzer bottle. Point it at the glass and fire. Very good for bottled-up aggression. Now mix it up, and look what you've got! If ever perfection came in a glass, this is it.

Now you look to me like one of those uncompromising souls, who just won't be satisfied with the basic. Don't worry. I've got just the thing for you. Yes sir. Plop in a scoop of vanilla ice cream, and presto: you've got what's known in the trade as a Black and White. Use vanilla instead of chocolate syrup and put in chocolate ice cream: that's a White and Black. If you're really adventurous, use root beer instead of seltzer and call it a Brown Cow. Actually you can call it whatever you like, but if you call it a Brown Cow, I'll know what you're talking about.

Tired of soda? No problem. We've got straight ice cream too. You could have Chocolate Chip, Chocolate Mocha Chip, Mocha Fudge Ripple, Pralines 'n Cream, Rocky Road, Tin Roof . . . I'm not making this up, you know.

Okay, I've got just the thing for you. The Magnum Opus, the *pièce de résistance*: the ice cream sundae.

Use the wildest ice cream you can dream of. Smother it in sauce: Marshmallow, Caramel, Hot Fudge, Walnut–Chocolate, Butterscotch, Apricot . . . Top it with crushed fruit, nuts and whipped cream until you can't see the ice cream. It might kill you, but you sure die happy.

Okay, what'll it be?'

Shawm Kreitzman, *Eats for Treats*, BBC

⊕ BANANA SPLITS

What's the ultimate ice cream fantasy? The banana split, of course. You split a banana (get it? Banana split?) and *smother* it in goodies: every flavour of ice cream you can think of, hot chocolate sauce, raspberry sauce, chopped nuts . . . wait a minute! Hold the phone! Has Sue K. gone completely *bananas* herself? Is she *nuts*?! This is supposed to be Slim Cuisine, remember?

Well, of course. Would I lead you astray? Bananas are the healthy eater's best friend: no fat, bursting with vitamins, minerals and lovely complex carbohydrate – a perfectly packaged, sweet and friendly, always accessible fruit. Split the exemplary fruit and smother it in Slim Cuisine ice creams and sorbets: vanilla, chocolate, mango, raspberry, strawberry, peach, pear, pineapple, whatever pleases you. Why not a little of each?

Blanket the bananas and their lavish ice creams and sorbets with Slim Cuisine Hot Chocolate Sauce, Raspberry Sauce and – instead of high-fat chopped nuts – sprinkle the whole thing with crumbled amaretti and Grape-Nuts cereal. Now *that's* a banana split!!

♡ To make a wonderful banana split that conforms to the Slim Cuisine weight *loss* regime, use fruit coulis only (no hot fudge sauce) and Slim Cuisine food processor ice creams sweetened with NutraSweet. Sprinkle the top of the banana split with Grape-Nuts cereal.

Cold Fruit Soups

Back in the early seventies, I cooked in a small bistro in Atlanta, Georgia. It was an innovative, quirky place with a devoted clientele, and I was given a free hand with menu planning (we changed the menu every day). I was fascinated at that time (as indeed I still am) with Hungarian food, and frequently offered a Hungarian dish among the evening's choices. Cold fruit soup, especially blueberry and cherry, were particular Hungarian favourites of mine and, when fresh blueberries or sour cherries were available, I'd offer one or the other of them among the soup choices. In those days, in Atlanta, cold soup was an oddity, to say the least. I *knew* people would be confused – at that time, *vichyssoise* was the only cold soup occasionally (very occasionally) encountered in Atlanta, and *gazpacho* was only a vague rumour – so each time cold fruit soup was featured on the menu, I'd write a careful explanation on the evening's hand-written menu sheet. 'Cold fruit soup is a terrific way to begin a meal,' I'd write. 'People

do, all the time, in Hungary. It's a *soup*, you see – and it's *cold*.'
'Yes,' I'd write, '*cold* fruit soup is sweet, but it's tart as well so that
– even though it is *cold* – it makes a lovely start to a meal.' My
menu exhortations worked pretty well: customers ordered the
soup. They may have regarded it as unusual but, on the whole,
they seemed to enjoy it. But still, despite my encyclopaedic
covering of the cold fruit soup story on the hand-written menu,
there were confusions. One evening a customer called me to his
table after he had finished his meal. He was feeling expansive, as
well-fed customers always do, but there was an underlying seed
of displeasure there, too. 'The trout,' he said, kissing his
fingertips and rolling his eyes toward heaven, 'it was the best I've
ever eaten. And the zucchini with walnuts . . . ' Words failed
him; the zucchini was just too remarkable to talk about appa-
rently. 'But the soup,' he beckoned me closer and dropped his
voice to a horrified whisper, 'the soup was ICE COLD!'

It was after that encounter that I instructed the waitresses, as
they were placing the soup on the table, to look each customer
straight in the eye and announce firmly and clearly, 'The soup is
supposed to be cold!'

The cold fruit soups in this collection are meant to be served
after dinner, for dessert, so confusion should be minimal. They
are good to eat, and beautiful to look at: perfect dinner party
desserts, in fact.

COLD BLUEBERRY SOUP WITH BLUEBERRY SORBET

Makes 1¼ pints/700 ml

This cold soup is meant to be served as dessert, with a scoop of
Blueberry Sorbet centred in each bowlful. The soup with its sorbet
is visually stunning, and usually brings gasps of delight from
dinner guests.

1 lb/450 g blueberries	1 cinnamon stick
15 fl oz/400 ml water	2 oz/50 g vanilla sugar
1 small lemon, sliced (remove pips)	(see page 16)
	Blueberry Sorbet (see below)

1   Combine the berries, water, lemon, cinnamon and sugar in a
    non-reactive saucepan. Bring to boil, reduce heat, and
    simmer for 10 minutes. Cool.
2   Remove the lemon slices and cinnamon stick. Purée the soup

in the liquidizer until very smooth and velvety. Pour into a jar and chill.

3   Stir chilled soup well. Pour into shallow soup plates, and put a scoop of sorbet in the centre of each.

♡ Omit the sugar. Sweeten to taste with NutraSweet after the soup has cooled.

♡ ⊕ ❋ BLUEBERRY SORBET

Makes 1½ pints/900 ml sorbet

If you use the Slim Cuisine food processor ice cream method (page 94) but substitute unsweetened fruit juice for the butter-milk, you end up with a beautiful instant sorbet. As with the ice creams, they may be eaten at once, or stored in the freezer for up to 1 hour.

12 oz/350 g frozen blueberries (see page 94 for the method for freezing berries)	*NutraSweet to taste*
	Approximately 4 fl oz/100 ml unsweetened apple juice
1 teaspoon natural vanilla essence	

1   Combine all the ingredients except the apple juice and NutraSweet in the food processor container. Pour in 2 fl oz/50 ml of the apple juice.

2   Process until the fruit is roughly chopped. Taste and add a bit of NutraSweet if necessary. Continue processing. Pour in the remaining juice as it processes. Stop and scrape down container as needed. When the mixture forms a smooth sorbet consistency, scrape into a container and freeze for up to 1 hour.

PEACH–RASPBERRY SOUP WITH PEACH SORBET

Makes 1¼ pints/700 ml

A store-cupboard version of cold fruit soup with sorbet. Although both components are made with tinned fruit there is absolutely no compromise of taste in the finished dish: this is a very, very special recipe.

1 tin (15 oz/425 g) sliced peaches,	*8 fl oz/225 ml sweet white wine*
* in natural juice*	*1 teaspoon natural vanilla essence*
1 tin (15 oz/425 g) Scottish	*1 cinnamon stick*
* raspberries, in natural juice*	*Slivered zest of ½ small lemon and*
1½ oz/40 g sugar	* ½ small orange*
1 tablespoon orange liqueur	*1 slice lemon (no pips)*
* (Cointreau or Grand Marnier)*	*Peach Sorbet (see below)*

1   Combine the fruits and their juices with all the remaining ingredients (except peach sorbet) in a non-reactive saucepan. Bring to a boil, then reduce the heat and simmer for 10 minutes. Cool

2   Remove the lemon slice and cinnamon stick. Purée the soup in the liquidizer or processor until very smooth, then push through a sieve. Pour into a jar and chill.

3   Stir the chilled soup well. Pour into shallow soup plates, and put a generous scoop of sorbet into the centre of each. Garnish with a mint leaf if you have any. Serve at once.

♡ Omit the sugar. Sweeten to taste with NutraSweet after the soup has cooled.

♡ ⏲ ❄ PEACH SORBET

Makes 1 pint/570 ml

If the peach slices are frozen in advance, this recipe – as with all Slim Cuisine food processor ice creams and sorbets – takes scant minutes to make.

1 tin (15 oz/425 g) sliced peaches	*NutraSweet as needed*
* in natural juice*	*A few drops fresh lemon juice*
½ teaspoon natural vanilla essence	

1   Drain peaches *very* well. Refrigerate the juices. Spread the drained peach slices out on a non-stick tray and freeze. When thoroughly frozen, put into a plastic bag and store in the freezer until needed.

2   Put the frozen peach slices in the container of the processor, along with the vanilla and 2 fl oz/50 ml of the peach juice. Process for a minute or so. Stop and scrape down the container. Turn the machine on again and process, gradually adding another 2–3 fl oz/50–75 ml peach juice and a few

drops of lemon juice as it processes. Stop, scrape down and taste. Add a little NutraSweet, and a bit more lemon juice as needed. Process until very smooth and fluffy. Scrape into a jug or container, and store in the freezer for up to an hour.

HOT AND COLD PINEAPPLE

Another 'hot as summer, cold as winter' extravaganza; this time, cubes of hot, rum-soaked pineapple, topped with scoops of juicy, freshly made pineapple sorbet.

1 large ripe pineapple, peeled and cored	4 tablespoons dark rum
1½–3 tablespoons light brown sugar (depending on the sweetness of the pineapple)	Pineapple Sorbet (see below)

1   Preheat the oven to 400°F, 200°C, Gas Mark 6.
2   Cut the peeled, cored pineapple into 1-inch/2.5-cm pieces. Put them in a shallow non-reactive baking dish.
3   Combine the sugar and rum in a saucepan. Bring to a boil, stirring occasionally. Boil for 1 minute. Pour the mixture over the pineapple and stir to combine. Cover and bake for 40 minutes.
4   Divide the hot pineapple among 4 goblets. Pour the hot juices over the pineapple and top each with a generous scoop of cold sorbet.

♡ Omit the sugar.

♡ ⊕ ❄ PINEAPPLE SORBET

This sorbet is *pure pineapple*. See page 94 for preparing and storing the frozen pineapple cubes. If the pineapple is tart, you may want to sweeten the sorbet with a bit of NutraSweet, but a truly ripe pineapple is usually sweet enough.

10 oz/275 g frozen pineapple cubes	2–3 fl oz/50–75 ml unsweetened pineapple juice
1 tablespoon each: natural vanilla essence and dark rum	

1   Combine the pineapple, vanilla, rum and 1 fl oz/25 ml of the
    juice in the processor container. Process until roughly chop-
    ped. Stop and scrape down the container.
2   Begin processing again. As it processes, pour in the remain-
    ing juice. When the mixture forms a sorbet consistency (you
    may have to stop and scrape it down another time or two),
    scrape into a container and store in the freezer for up to an
    hour.

⊕ BANANA–GINGER SORBET

Yields ¾ pint/400 ml

I have to call this a sorbet because it contains *no* dairy product at
all, but it is really rich and creamy enough to be called an ice
cream. Try this sorbet on Grilled Bananas and Rum (page 52). The
sensation of eating the hot, tender bananas in their caramelized
juices sizzling under a scoop of this creamy, rich, slowly melting
cold sorbet is indescribable.

---

10 oz/275 g frozen banana slices	*Juice of 1 orange*
(see page 94)	*½ teaspoon natural vanilla essence*
1 lump crystallized ginger, diced	

---

1   Place the frozen banana slices in the container of the food
    processor. Add the ginger, orange juice and vanilla essence.
2   Turn on the processor and let it run until the mixture is
    beautifully smooth and creamy. Stop and scrape down the
    sides if necessary.

❄ ORANGE CREAMSICLE

Orange Creamsicle is based on a remembered childhood treat
from the 'Good Humor Man'; the white-uniformed ice cream
vendor who pedalled his cart down neighbourhood streets,
ringing his little bell. Like so many Pavlov's dogs, the neighbourhood kids would appear, small change clenched in their fists.
Orange Creamsicle was vanilla ice cream encased in orange
sherbet and impaled on a stick. Ever since, I've loved that
combination of flavours. This is an adult version, much tarter
than what I remember from forty years ago, but it successfully
combines vanilla creaminess with orange iciness.

2½ tins partially thawed orange juice concentrate	1 teaspoon natural vanilla essence
4 tablespoons sugar	½ teaspoon slivered orange zest (see page 34)
2–4 tablespoons NutraSweet (to taste)	9½ fl oz/284 ml buttermilk

1   Combine all the ingredients in the food processor. Process until very smooth.
2   Freeze in an ice cream maker according to the manufacturer's directions. Store in the freezer. Serve in scoops, as you would sorbet or ice cream.

❄ *Variation*: Grapefruit Creamsicle

Prepare as Orange Creamsicle, but substitute grapefruit juice concentrate for the orange juice concentrate. You will probably need to add more sweetener.

MELON SORBET

An icy and refreshing essence of summer. Serve in melon halves or frozen in hollowed-out orange shells. Or serve in a goblet of apple–raspberry juice.

8 oz/225 g honeydew melon, cubed	1½–2 tablespoons sugar
8 oz/225 g watermelon, cubed, seeds removed	Fresh lime juice (approximately 1 teaspoon)
1 tablespoon orange liqueur (Cointreau or Grand Marnier)	Apple–raspberry juice (see note, page 109)

1   Combine the melon cubes, their juices, the orange liqueur and the sugar in a non-reactive bowl. Mash together with a potato masher. Pour the mixture into a measuring jug. Add apple–raspberry juice until the mixture measures 1 pint/570 ml. Liquidize to a rough purée. Add lime juice (the exact amount depends on the sweetness of the melons).
2   Process in an electric ice cream maker according to the manufacturer's directions.

Note: Some supermarkets sell bottled apple–raspberry juice, or you can make your own by combining natural (unsweetened) apple juice with the drained juices from thawed frozen raspberries. Use the raspberries themselves to make Raspberry Coulis (page 98).

♡ Replace the sugar with NutraSweet.

Let Them Eat Cheesecake

'Cheesecake is excess. Perhaps it is that excess that arouses such strong passions . . . You know, we know, everybody knows that each little bit of the stuff will add pounds to our bodies. Somewhere up in the sky a little cholesterol counter is going haywire, and we don't care.'

Bovbjerg and Iggers, *The Joy of Cheesecake*

Cheesecake

When I think about cheesecake, I think about extravagant creaminess in a crumb crust. Classic cheesecake, in the New York Deli tradition, is extravagantly creamy all right: butter, cream cheese, sour cream, double cream, whole eggs and extra yolks – in other words fat upon fat. I learned about cheesecake years ago from the man in charge of such things at the legendary Carnegie Deli in New York City, so I am steeped in tradition up to my neck. 'Cheesecake must have a crumb crust,' instructed the cheesecake maestro. 'A pastry crust would interfere with the cheesecake's remarkable richness.' I still agree with those words of wisdom: a crumb crust is the only possible one to bestow beneath a cheesecake, but I have switched from a butter-bound crust to an egg-white-bound one, and the crumbs I use are now low-fat ones.

Mr Weiner also cautioned me to avoid smothering a cheesecake under thick, gelatinous fruit toppings, and I have heeded his advice, succumbing only to the occasional discreetly scattered strawberry or mandarin slice in the name of garnish. It is in the filling itself that I have completely broken with tradition. Instead of the classic killer-combo of egg yolks, creams, and cream cheese, I now use a whipped quark mixture. Another departure: classic cheesecakes are baked, my new versions are not. Gelatin-bound unbaked cheesecakes are horribly rubbery; therefore not a speck of gelatin lurks in these creamy beauties. Most cheesecakes are mission-oriented: they are programmed to seduce you with their creamy excesses, then – as you swoon with the deliciousness of it all – rush to expand your fat stores with a rapid efficency that will break your heart. Why not just rub great gobbets of the stuff directly on to your thighs, and let it go at that? Forget the killer cheesecakes – Slim Cuisine is here to change your life.

CRUMB CRUSTS

Choose the crust you want for your cheesecake: Grape-Nuts, amaretti (almond flavour), or half and half.

1   **Plain Crumb Crust**: Preheat the oven to 350°F, 180°C, Gas Mark 4. Put 5 oz/150 g of Grape-Nuts cereal into a bowl. Lightly beat 2 egg whites. With 2 spoons, toss together the Grape-Nuts and the egg white until the former is thoroughly coated with the latter. Pour the mixture into a 10-inch/25-cm non-stick, round flan tin. With the back of a dessert spoon or a serving spoon, spread the Grape-Nuts evenly over the

bottom and up the sides to form a thin layer. Bake for 5–7 minutes. Cool. When cool, spread and swirl the cheesecake mixture over the crust. Chill for several hours or overnight. During the chilling process, the crust will soften to just the right consistency.

2   **Amaretti Crumb Crust**: Preheat the oven to 350°F, 180°C, Gas Mark 4. Put 5 oz/150 g of amaretti biscuits into a plastic bag and – with a rolling pin or kitchen mallet – reduce them to coarse crumbs. Lightly beat 1 egg white. In a bowl, toss the crumbs and egg white together until the former is thoroughly coated with the latter. Put the mixture into a 10-inch/25-cm non-stick round flan tin. With the back of a dessert spoon or serving spoon, spread it evenly over the bottom and up the sides. Bake for 7–10 minutes. Cool on rack.

3   **Half and Half Crumb Crust**: Make the crust as above, but use 2½ oz/60 g amaretti biscuits, 2½ oz/60 g Grape-Nuts cereal and 2 egg whites.

'Wildly excessive, very wet, intensely sweet, heavy, thickly studded with candied fruit.'
Description of a cheesecake in
Seymour Britchky, *The Restaurants of New York*

RUM–RAISIN CHEESECAKE

Makes 1 10-inch/25-cm cheesecake

In this cheesecake, and a few of the ones that follow, sweetness is provided by pulverized raisins or currants, and a bit of Nutra-Sweet. Sweetness is very much a matter of taste; you must taste the mixture and adjust the amount of NutraSweet to your liking.

6 generous tablespoons raisins	28 oz/800 g quark or very low-fat
4 tablespoons dark rum	curd cheese (4 small cartons)
1 teaspoon natural vanilla essence	NutraSweet to taste
5 tablespoons water	Half and half crumb crust
Finely slivered zest of 1 small	(above)
orange and 1 small lemon	
(see page 34)	

1   Combine the raisins, rum, vanilla, water and zest in a small pan. Simmer until the raisins are plump and the liquid has reduced to ½ tablespoon. Cool.

2   Combine the raisin mixture and the quark in the processor

container. Process for a moment or so. Taste, and sweeten as needed with NutraSweet. Process until fluffy. By the time you have finished processing, the raisins should be almost puréed.

3 Spread and swirl the mixture in the cheesecake crust. Chill for several hours or overnight.

Amaretti Biscuits

Amaretti biscuits are crunchy almond-flavoured meringues from Italy. They can be bought in pretty red and white tins; when the biscuits are gone, the tins are useful for storage. Amaretti, although almond-flavoured, contain no high-fat almonds; the flavour comes from apricot pits. The biscuits are very useful in crumb crusts, and in recipes where you want both almond flavour and crunch, they make a good garnish too. Try them crumbled on to servings of Slim Cuisine Peach Food Processor Ice Cream (page 94).

AMARETTI CHEESECAKE

Makes 1 10-inch/25-cm cheesecake

This is one of the most elegant cheesecakes in the collection – very appropriate for special occasions.

6 generous tablespoons raisins	*28 oz/800 g quark or very low-fat*
1 teaspoon natural vanilla essence	*curd cheese (4 small cartons)*
1½ teaspoons almond essence	*NutraSweet to taste*
2 tablespoons brandy	*Amaretti crumb crust (page 114)*
8 tablespoons water	*1 amaretti biscuit, crumbled*
	½ tablespoon Grape-Nuts cereal

1 Combine the raisins, vanilla and almond essence, brandy and water in a small pan. Simmer until the raisins are plump and the liquid has reduced to ½–1 tablespoon. Cool thoroughly.
2 Combine the raisin mixture and the quark in the processor container. Process for a moment or so. Taste and sweeten as needed with NutraSweet. Process until fluffy, and the raisins are almost puréed.
3 Spread and swirl the mixture over the amaretti crust. Combine the crumbed amaretti biscuit and the Grape-Nuts. Sprinkle evenly over the cheesecake. Chill for several hours or overnight.

SHERRY–CURRANT CHEESECAKE

Makes 1 10-inch/25-cm cheesecake

6 tablespoons dried currants	*28 oz/800 g quark or very low-fat*
6 tablespoons cream sherry	*curd cheese (4 small cartons)*
3 tablespoons water	*NutraSweet to taste*
1 tablespoon natural vanilla essence	*Plain crumb crust (page 113)*

1   Combine the currants, sherry, water and vanilla in a small pan. Simmer until the currants are plump and very syrupy, and the liquid has cooked down to ½–1 tablespoon. Cool thoroughly.
2   With a rubber scraper, scrape the currants and all their syrupy juices into the processor container. Add the quark. Process until almost smooth. Taste. Add NutraSweet to taste if needed. Process until very smooth and fluffy, and the currants are totally puréed.
3   Swirl and spread the mixture over the crumb crust. Chill until needed.

PINEAPPLE CHEESECAKE

Makes 1 10-inch/25-cm cheesecake

Tinned crushed pineapple beaten into quark makes one of the most pleasing cheesecakes of all. The filling itself can be used to make a *coeur à la crème* (see page 53) if you are in a pineapple mood but not a cheesecake one.

2 tins (15½ oz/435 g each) crushed	*NutraSweet to taste*
pineapple in natural juice	*Half and half crust (page 114)*
28 oz/800 g quark (4 small cartons)	*½ tablespoon light brown sugar*
1 teaspoon natural vanilla essence	*mixed with ½ tablespoon Grape-*
1 tablespoon dark rum	*Nuts cereal*

1   Drain the pineapple in a sieve set over a bowl. Press down on the pineapple pulp to extract as much juice as possible. (Save the juice for another use.)
2   Combine *half* the pineapple, the quark, vanilla and rum in the container of the food processor. Process until very smooth and fluffy. Add NutraSweet to taste, and process until blended.
3   Gently fold in the remaining pineapple with a rubber spatula.

4   Line a sieve with muslin or a jelly bag, and place it over a deep bowl. Scrape the cheese mixture into the sieve. Refrigerate and allow to drain for 1–2 hours.
5   When the pineapple–cheese is firm and well drained, swirl and spread it into the crust. Sprinkle the top evenly with the sugar–Grape-Nuts mixture. Cover and chill overnight.

♡ Omit the ½ tablespoon of sugar topping, and the amaretti crust. Use a plain crumb crust (page 113) instead.

PUMPKIN CHEESECAKE

Makes 1 10-inch/25-cm cheesecake

Puréed pumpkin, raisins, rum, maple syrup and spices beaten into quark make a splendid filling for an autumn or winter cheesecake. Cooked puréed pumpkin is available in tins from many supermarkets. To prepare pumpkin purée from fresh pumpkins: buy small pumpkins, cut the flesh into cubes (discard the stringy pulp), and steam until very tender. Drain well and purée in a liquidizer or blender.

6 generous tablespoons raisins	*Pinch ground allspice*
Slivered zest of 1 lemon	*Pinch ground ginger*
2 tablespoons dark rum	*Pinch ground nutmeg*
6 tablespoons water	*½ teaspoon ground cinnamon*
1 teaspoon natural vanilla essence	*2 tablespoons maple syrup*
1 tin (15 oz/425 g) puréed cooked	*NutraSweet to taste*
* pumpkin*	*Half and half crumb crust (page 114)*
28 oz/800 g quark, or very low-fat	*½ tablespoon brown sugar*
* curd cheese (4 small cartons)*	*1 tablespoon Grape-Nuts cereal*

1   Combine the raisins, lemon zest, dark rum, water and vanilla in a small pan. Simmer until the raisins are plump and the liquid has reduced to ½–1 tablespoon. Cool.
2   In the food processor, combine the cooled raisins with all the remaining ingredients except the crumb crust, brown sugar and Grape-Nuts. Process until almost smooth. Taste. Add NutraSweet to taste. Process until very smooth and fluffy (the raisins should be almost totally puréed). Line a sieve with muslin or a jelly bag, and place over a deep bowl. Scrape the pumpkin–cheese mixture into the sieve. Refriger-ate for 1 hour to drain.
3   Swirl and spread the pumpkin-cheese filling over the crust.

Combine the brown sugar and Grape-Nuts cereal. Sprinkle evenly over the top of the cheesecake. Chill for several hours or overnight.

MANDARIN–GINGER CHEESECAKE

Makes 1 10-inch/25.5-cm cheesecake

I love the bracing gingery bite of this cheesecake, but if you are not a ginger fan, leave out the crystallized ginger and enjoy the orange flavour on its own.

2 tins (11 oz/298 g each) mandarins in natural juice	*1 tablespoon orange liqueur (Cointreau or Grand Marnier)*
35 oz/975 g quark (5 small cartons)	*NutraSweet to taste*
1 teaspoon natural vanilla essence	*Half and half crumb crust (page 114)*
½ oz/10 g crystallized ginger, diced	*Crystallized ginger to decorate*

1 Drain the mandarins in a sieve set over a bowl. Press down on the mandarin pulp to extract as much juice as possible. (Save the juice for another use.)

2 Combine *half* the mandarins with the quark, vanilla, crystallized ginger and orange liqueur in the container of a food processor. Process until very smooth and fluffy. Add NutraSweet to taste, and process until blended.

3 Gently fold in the remaining mandarins with a rubber spatula. (Save a few for decoration.)

4 Line a sieve with muslin or a jelly bag, and place it over a deep bowl. Scrape the cheese mixture into the sieve. Refrigerate and allow to drain for 1–2 hours.

5 When the mandarin–cheese is firm and well drained, swirl and spread it into the crust. Cover and chill overnight. Garnish with drained, blotted-dry mandarin slices and slivers of diced crystallized ginger.

SWEET POTATO CREAM PIE

Makes 1 10-inch/25-cm pie

Have you ever had a baked sweet potato? If not, I suggest you drop everything, rush to the market, and grab a bagful to take home. For an utterly satisfying, simple sweet meal, prick a sweet potato in several places and bake directly on the oven shelf for 1

118

hour, or until it is tender and sputtering with leaking, caramelized juices. With a fork, perforate the top of the potato lengthwise and crosswise and squeeze, so that the sweet flesh comes surging up through the dotted lines. Lightly mash the flesh right in the skin and top with a generous dollop of Honeyed Vanilla or Almond Cream (page 81). Or mash the flesh with a bit of honey or maple syrup, a bit of cinnamon and some fromage frais.

If you want a sweet potato treat that is somewhat less primitive and immediate than plainly baked, try this creamy pie. During blueberry season, squirrel quantities of the berries away in your freezer – then you will be able to garnish your wedge of sweet potato pie with a generous dollop of Blueberry Compôte.

After preparing this spectacular dessert, you will be left with the baked sweet potato skins. Cut into strips, quickly grilled, and served with Honeyed Vanilla Cream, they make a sybaritic snack.

---

3 large sweet potatoes
½–¾ oz/10–15 g crystallized
   ginger, diced small
½ teaspoon cinnamon
1½–2 tablespoons dark rum
2 tablespoons runny honey
Finely slivered zest of ½ lemon
1 teaspoon natural vanilla essence

28 oz/800 g quark or very low-fat
   curd cheese (4 small cartons)
1 tin crushed pineapple in natural
   juice, very well drained in a
   nylon sieve
Half and half crumb crust (page 114)
Blueberry Compôte (optional)
   (page 75)

---

1   Preheat oven to 400°F, 200°C, Gas Mark 6. Pierce the sweet potatoes in several places with a fork or thin skewer. Bake directly on the oven shelf for 1 hour, or until the potatoes are very tender, and leaking caramellized juices.

2   Cut each potato in half. Scoop out the potato flesh into a bowl. Mash well with a potato masher. (You need ¾ pint/400 ml mashed sweet potato. Save any extra for another use.) Put the potatoes into the container of the processor with all the remaining ingredients except the pineapple, crumb crust and Blueberry Compôte. Process until very smooth and fluffy.

3   Press down on the pineapple in the sieve with the back of a large spoon, so that the fruit is as dry as possible. With the back of the spoon, spread the pineapple evenly over the crust. With a rubber spatula, spread and swirl the sweet potato mixture over the pineapple. Cover and chill. Serve wedges of this pie with Blueberry Compôte, if desired.

Chocoholics Unite

'The smell of chocolate bubbling over and slightly burning is one of the most beautiful smells in the world. It is subtle and comforting and it is rich. One tiny drop perfumes a room as nothing else.'

Laurie Colwin, *Home Cooking*

Chocolate

The Aztecs believed that Quetzalcoatl, the God of wind and fertility – a fierce-looking spirit if his turquoise-studded mask is anything to go by – presented cocoa to mankind. By all accounts Montezuma and his crowd consumed chocolate as a potent, ceremonial drink made from cocoa paste, but the exact form of that drink is open to debate. My reading of the evidence assures me that the chocolate drink of that time and place (pre-Columbian Central America) was not the cup-of-cocoa cosiness it is today. But was the Aztec drink sweetened with cane sugar, scented with vanilla, spiced with cinnamon, or knocked back straight, bitter and potent? The history books disagree. Centuries after Montezuma and the Aztec Empire – in 1984 in fact – I came across an Aztec chocolate vendor in the sprawling, colourful market in Cholula, Mexico. She stood behind a vat of murky brown liquid, beating it into froth with a beautifully carved *molinillo* (wooden chocolate beater). The liquid was *chocolatl*, the descendant of Montezuma's old favourite. The *chocolatl* woman sold either a serving of the foam, scooped from the top of her vat, or a serving (for another peso or two) of the chocolate water. It was scooped or ladled into a beautiful red and black lacquered bowl, and one gulped or drank, acquiring a spectacular chocolate moustache in the process, and then returned the bowl. Another woman wandered the market selling solid chocolate in the form of incised flat discs. The sweetened chocolate was grainy, crumbly and flavoured with cinnamon. Yes, Montezuma consumed a form of chocolate, but he would never have recognized these discs as his old standby. Yet those discs – the ultimate in modernity and technological chocolate achievement in contrast with the pre-Columbian cocoa paste – seemed primitive and coarse to me, who grew up on the creamy-smooth excesses of Tobler, Cadbury and Hershey.

Both Columbus and Cortes, in the early sixteenth century, sent cocoa beans back to Spain. Chocolate didn't *immediately* become the toast of Europe; there was the usual distrust and paranoia that new foodstuffs, hot off the boat from the New World, engendered. According to Waverley Root, in his *Food Encyclopaedia*, 'France regarded it askance as at best a barbarous product and at worse a noxious drug.' But it didn't take all that long for chocolate to become very popular indeed among the aristocracy in Spain (Spain tried very hard to monopolize its trade), and finally in the rest of Western Europe. At first, chocolate was taken as a drink (as it would remain for 200 years), sweetened with sugar and flavoured with vanilla. The English added milk to it in 1700.

Towards the end of the century French and Dutch processors found a way to defat the chocolate liquor and manufacture a powder: Conrad Van Houten, a Dutchman, patented this process in 1828. By the mid nineteenth century, a solid eating chocolate was being manufactured by adding very finely ground sugar to cocoa butter. In 1876 milk chocolate was deveoped in Switzerland, and this became its most popular form.

There is no doubt that chocolate, its deep bitterness tempered by sugar, is one of the most compelling and delicious foodstuffs in the world. Why should it be a surprise that, over the centuries, chocolate has been considered an aphrodisiac? It's not just that chocolate is delicious, there really is something erotic about it: chocolate speaks to you in places you didn't even know you had. If you share a cosy cup of cocoa with your spouse or significant other just before bedtime, surely when bedtime arrives, you will be doing more than just peacefully dozing.

Chocolate begins as cocoa beans encased in the pods of the cocoa tree; when the pods are ripe they are cut from the tree and chopped open. The beans and their surrounding pulp are piled into special boxes, covered with leaves and left to ferment. Without fermentation the beans will not develop their characteristic and intoxicating chocolate aroma. Cocoa beans are very high in saturated fat (cocoa butter). During processing the cocoa butter is removed. Later, it is put back, or – in some cases – vegetable fat is put back, and the cocoa butter is used for other things – cosmetics for instance. Either way, solid chocolate has a high fat content. Even cocoa powder usually has fat added back. Fortunately, excellent low-fat cocoa powder is available, and this is what you should use for Slim Cuisine chocolate desserts (see Mail Order Guide, page 133.) I find that the taste of low-fat cocoa is more intense than the higher-fat kind, therefore the desserts you prepare from the low-fat powder will satisfy in the deep recesses of your chocolate-loving soul.

OLD-FASHIONED DARK CHOCOLATE PUDDING

Serves 2–4

Dear chocoholics – if you have recovered from the intensity of the Chocolate Sorbet experience (page 94) I have another one for you. When I say *Dark Chocolate* Pudding, I'm not kidding. You will fall into this one and not come up for days. I experimented with many versions of chocolate pudding and this – very simple to make – is the ultimate. I cooked this pudding on television and it engendered over 25,000 viewer responses.

4 tablespoons low-fat unsweetened cocoa powder (see Mail Order Guide, page 133) 4 tablespoons caster sugar	2 tablespoons cornflour Tiny pinch of salt ¾ pint/400 ml skimmed milk

1   Put all the ingredients into the container of a liquidizer, and blend until *very* smooth.
2   Rinse a heavy, non-stick saucepan with cold water. Pour out the water, but do not dry the saucepan (this helps reduce scorching). Pour the chocolate–milk mixture into the pan. Heat on medium heat, stirring, until it begins to bubble strenuously. As you stir do not scrape the bottom: if any scorching does occur on the bottom of the saucepan, you do not want to stir the scorched bits into the pudding. Continue stirring and cooking for 1 minute. Remove from the heat.
3   Immediately pour into glass dessert goblets. Cover with cling film and refrigerate until serving time.

Taste Them if You Dare

Many of my chocolate recipes – the Chocolate Pudding and the Chocolate Almond Pie, the Chocolate Sorbet and the Chocolate Roulade – were designed for serious worshippers of the noble cocoa bean. Those who prefer wimpy milk chocolate, who like their chocolate diluted, who want it pale brown and heavily sweetened, may suffer shocks to their system. These recipes produce dark, bittersweet, and emotion-engaging desserts. One does not toy with these puddings in a desultory fashion while sharing chit-chat with one's dinner party companions or while watching mindless flim-flam on the telly. Take the first bite: the only response is stunned silence while the dense, deep taste and texture wraps itself around your palate. I've seen it happen time and time again – the silence, the slowly widening eyes, the dawning appreciation of the overwhelming *chocolatiness* of it all. So taste them if you dare. It is not an experience to take lightly.

CHOCOLATE ALMOND PIE

Is it Valentine's Day? Your best friend's birthday? Do you have the urge to do something wonderful for someone you love? Perhaps the urge is to do something wonderful for *yourself*. *Do it!*

125

Make this pie and bestow it tenderly upon those who need it. Every once in a while a trendy restaurant will offer a totally over-the-top chocolate dessert they have dubbed 'Death by Chocolate' or 'Chocolate Decadence'. They are not far off, either: the butterfat and cocoa butter levels in such concoctions make such names perfectly apt. But with my Chocolate Almond Pie there is no need to fight your conscience; this one gives you the 'Decadence' without the 'Death'.

Old-fashioned Dark Chocolate Pudding (see previous recipe)
Amaretti crumb crust or Half and half crumb crust (page 114)
1   amaretti biscuit, crushed

Spread and swirl the chocolate pudding over the amaretti crust. Sprinkle the crushed amaretti over the top. Chill for several hours or overnight.

> 'The Aztecs used the cocoa bean as a currency, and the Mayans did likewise. In fact, the Mayans even had trouble with "counterfeits". It seems that Mayan con-men filled hollowed beans with dirt and passed them off as the real thing.'
> Robert Hendrickson, *Lewd Food*

❄ CHOCOLATE ROULADE

Serves 4–6

One of my favourite Slim Cuisine recipes is the Dark Chocolate Soufflé from *Slim Cuisine: A Second Helping*. Here is that soufflé in another guise: baked flat on a silicone paper-lined baking sheet, spread with a luxurious filling, and rolled like a Swiss roll.

Soufflé Base

9 tablespoons caster sugar
9 tablespoons unsweetened low-fat cocoa (see Mail Order Guide, page 133)
9 egg whites, at room temperature

Pinch of cream of tartar
1½ teaspoons of natural vanilla essence
1½ teaspoons dark rum
Icing sugar

1   Preheat the oven to 350°F, 180°C, Gas Mark 4.
2   Line a non-stick baking sheet (13 × 9inches/33 × 23 cm) with silicone baking paper. Set aside.
3   Sift together all the sugar (except about 2 tablespoons) with all the cocoa. Set aside.
4   In an electric mixer, beat the egg whites with the cream of tartar until foamy. At highest speed, continue beating, adding the remaining 2 tablespoons of plain sugar a little at a time, until the whites hold stiff peaks.
5   With a rubber spatula, fold the sugar–cocoa mixture into the beaten whites. Fold in the vanilla and rum.
6   Gently and evenly spread the mixture on to the prepared baking sheet. Bake for 20–30 minutes (a toothpick should test *almost* clean). Cool the pan on a rack.
7   Spread a clean tea towel on your work surface. Cover with a sheet of waxed or greaseproof paper. Sprinkle evenly with icing sugar. When thoroughly cooled, turn the roulade base out on to the paper and peel off the silicone paper.
8   Spread with filling. Starting from the long edge, roll the roulade base like a Swiss roll. Use the tea towel to help you roll it. It may crack a bit, but it doesn't matter. Chill until needed. Serve in slices, with Raspberry Coulis if desired.

Possible Fillings
1   Banana Cream (page 52)
2   Strawberry Cream (page 54)
3   Any of the Chestnut Creams (page 72)

CHOCOLATE SOUFFLÉ

Serves 6

It doesn't seem fair to mention the incredible Slim Cuisine Chocolate Soufflé (as I have done in the introduction to the previous recipe) and then not provide the recipe. So here it is with its Chocolate Torte variation, reprinted from *Slim Cuisine: A Second Helping*.

---

9 tablespoons caster sugar
9 tablespoons unsweetened, fat-reduced cocoa (see Mail Order Guide, page 133)
9 egg whites, at room temperature

Pinch of cream of tartar
1½ teaspoons of natural vanilla essence
1½ teaspoons dark rum

---

1   Preheat the oven to 350°F, 180°C, Gas Mark 4.
2   Sift together all the sugar (except about 2 tablespoons) with all the cocoa. Set aside.
3   In an electric mixer, beat the egg whites with the cream of tartar until foamy. Continue beating at highest speed adding the remaining 2 tablespoons of plain sugar a little at a time, until the whites hold stiff peaks.
4   With a rubber spatula, fold the sugar–cocoa mixture into the beaten whites. Fold in the vanilla and rum.
5   Pile the egg white mixture into a 5½–6-pint/3.1–3.4-litre soufflé dish. Bake in the centre of the oven (remove the top shelf first) for 30–40 minutes. Serve at once.

Variation: Fudgy Chocolate Torte

To make a chocolate cake, follow the recipe above but use a 10-inch/25.5-cm non-stick flan tin instead of a soufflé dish and bake for 20–30 minutes. If you bake it too long it will be dry. (A skewer inserted near the middle should emerge not quite clean.) Remove from the oven and let cool on a rack. Cut and serve right from the tin.

REVERSE CHOCOLATE CHIP COOKIES

Makes 20

A friend from America – a dietitian – sent me a nice letter commenting on how successful she has been in changing her cooking habits from ordinary ones to Slim Cuisine ones. But she ended on a wistful note: 'Now if you could just invent a low-fat chocolate chip cookie, Terry [her husband] would be perfectly happy.' So here is my contribution to Terry's happiness – a chocolate meringue with bits in it. In a traditional chocolate chip cookie, the cookie is plain, the bits are chocolate. Here, it's the cookie that's chocolate, and the 'bits', plain.

3 egg whites, at room temperature	*4 tablespoons fat-reduced cocoa,*
Pinch of cream of tartar and salt	*sifted (see Mail Order Guide,*
5 oz/150 g sugar	*page 133)*
1 teaspoon natural vanilla essence	*10 fl oz/300 ml unsweetened puffed*
	rice cereal

1   Preheat the oven to 225°F, 120°C, Gas Mark 1.
2   Beat the egg whites with the cream of tartar and salt until foamy. Increase speed. Beat, adding the sugar 1–2 table-

Irresistible sweets: clockwise from bottom: fruit pizza, orange-lychee
bread pudding; sweet potato pie with blueberry compôte; honeyed cream.

Can she bake a cherry pie? Of course she can! Right to left:
cherry-peach flan, raspberry-pear flan.

spoons at a time, until the whites are shiny and stiff and hold firm peaks. Fold in the vanilla, cocoa and unsweetened puffed rice.

3   Line 2 baking sheets with silicon paper. Drop the batter on the sheets by the ½ teaspoonful, 1 inch/2.5cm apart. Bake for 45 minutes.

4   Turn the oven off. Leave the cookies in the oven for at *least* 3 hours. (Overnight is better.) Do not open the door until the time is up.

CHOCOLATE ALMOND CHEWIES

Makes 20

This is called recycling. Any old meringue cookies you have around the house can be crumbled, mixed with egg white and Grape-Nuts cereal, and baked until crunchy. If you wish, make a thumbprint depression in each before baking. Then, before serving, fill the depression with Banana Cream (page 52), Strawberry Cream (page 54), or one of the Chestnut Creams (page 72–73).

---

3 oz/75 g amaretti biscuits, crushed
1½ oz/40 g Reverse Chocolate Chip
*   Cookies (see previous recipe),*
*   crushed (6–8 cookies)*

½ oz/10 g Grape-Nuts cereal
2 egg whites

---

1   Preheat oven to 375°F, 190°C, Gas Mark 5.
2   Combine all the ingredients in a bowl.
3   Drop the mixture on to a non-stick baking tray by the teaspoonful. Bake in the oven for 20–30 minutes until dry and crispy (timing depends on the humidity). Store in an airtight tin.

CHOCOLATE MERINGUES

Makes 100

These meringues don't *rise* like little soufflés, in fact – if the atmosphere is humid or if it is rainy – they may collapse somewhat in the baking, but that's nothing to worry about. These are little cookies (okay – biscuits), so flat is fine.

3 egg whites, at room temperature	1 teaspoon natural vanilla essence
Pinch of cream of tartar and salt	4 tablespoons low-fat unsweetened
5 oz/150 g sugar	cocoa, sifted (see Mail Order Guide, page 133)

1   Preheat the oven to 225°F, 120°C, Gas Mark 1.
2   Beat the egg whites with the cream of tartar and salt until foamy. Increase speed. Beat, adding the sugar 1–2 table-spoons at a time, until the whites are shiny and stiff and hold firm peaks. Fold in the vanilla and cocoa.
3   Line 2 baking sheets with greaseproof paper. Drop the batter on sheets by the ½ teaspoonful, 1 inch/2.5cm apart. Bake for 45 minutes.
4   Turn the oven off. Leave the meringues in the oven for at least 3 hours. (They can stay in overnight.) Do not open the door until the time is up.

'But in the barrel of supplies was a wooden pail of chocolates, bell-shaped, black grocery chocolates, thinly coated with this new delicious substance, and filled with white cream candy, which was soft, but not sticky. Two of these were our portion and having eaten one, and found it to be like something one would dream of, but never taste, I tried to keep my second one to help me to meet some of life's vicissitudes. I might be crossed in love, as the years rolled on, or lose my character, or my money, and I knew this piece of magic, held tightly in my hand, would comfort me, for one moment at least, though all the world went wrong.'
Nellie L. McClung, *Clearing in the West*

Chestnut Cream Filled Biscuits

Several years ago I flew to the States for a visit carrying a dozen boxes of Gypsy Creams with me for an English friend living in America who couldn't live another day without his favourite cream-filled chocolate biscuits. On the way back to England, I carried a dozen bags of Oreos for an American friend living in England who couldn't live another day without *her* favourite cream-filled chocolate cookies. I guess cream-filled chocolate biscuits/cookies are a hot item. Hell, what do I mean I *guess*? I *know* they are. I suffer occasional severe twinges myself. Of course, I assuage those twinges with *Slim Cuisine* cream-filled chocolate doodads. At this point in my life, I wouldn't give a Gypsy Cream or an Oreo a second glance.

The method couldn't be simpler. Prepare a batch of Chocolate Meringues (page 129) and a batch of Chestnut Cream or Coffee–Chocolate Cream (pages 72, 73) and introduce them to each other; that is to say, sandwich some of the cream in between two meringues. Make this ½–1 hour before serving, to give the ingredients a chance to get to know each other. The meringue takes on a wonderful very slightly gooey texture during the wait. But if you can't wait, slap them together and eat them at once.

Chocolate Fondue

Chocolate Fondue was invented in New York in the early sixties by a Swiss-American restaurateur named Conrad Egli. In those days, my husband and I used to dine at Mr Egli's restaurant, the Chalet Suisse, on gala occasions. It was our practice to eat veal in cream sauce, wild mushrooms, what I remember as the best creamed spinach in the world, and roesti potatoes, while all around us, diners dipped and dunked hunks of meat into pots of bubbling oil. At that time, in the US, fondue was not the craze it was to become: this was before the era when every new bride received at least four fondue sets. We thought that fondue was moderately interesting but the veal was so much more delicious. But then Mr Egli invented the chocolate version. If you ordered this amazing dessert at the Chalet Suisse, a small vat of molten chocolate (milk chocolate Toblerone bars melted into double cream and kirsch and stirred until smooth) was placed on the

131

table. Tiny profiteroles that the austere and elegant Mr Egli made every morning with his own hands were provided as well. The idea was to spear a mini-profiterole on your fondue fork, sweep it slowly through the thick molten chocolate, and then eat, lingeringly, usually uttering sighs and groans as you did so. We still felt that we weren't in dire need of chunks of meat dabbled in boiling oil, but oh! that chocolate fondue. The happy news is that you can have a perfectly splendid Slim Cuisine chocolate fondue. Provide each diner with a vat of Hot Chocolate Sauce (page 96) and cubes of 1-or 2-day-old Angel Cake (page 60). If you wish, serve – in season – ripe strawberries as well. Spear, swirl, dunk, devour. Isn't life wonderful?

Mail Order Guide

For Cambridge Slim Cuisine low-fat unsweetened cocoa powder and information on other hard-to-find ingredients, write to:

Cambridge Slim Cuisine Products
202A Brakey Road
Corby
Northants
NN17 1LU

Tel: 0536 401500

Index